Erotic Love Poems

of

GREECE

AND

ROME

Erotic Love Poems

of

GREECE

AND

ROME

❧

A COLLECTION OF NEW TRANSLATIONS

BY

STEPHEN BERTMAN

NAL NEW AMERICAN LIBRARY

New American Library
Published by New American Library, a division of
Penguin Group (USA) Inc., 375 Hudson Street, New York,
New York 10014, USA
Penguin Group (Canada), 10 Alcorn Avenue, Toronto,
Ontario M4V 3B2, Canada (a division of Pearson Penguin Canada Inc.)
Penguin Books Ltd., 80 Strand, London WC2R 0RL, England
Penguin Ireland, 25 St. Stephen's Green, Dublin 2,
Ireland (a division of Penguin Books Ltd.)
Penguin Group (Australia), 250 Camberwell Road, Camberwell, Victoria 3124,
Australia (a division of Pearson Australia Group Pty. Ltd.)
Penguin Books India Pvt. Ltd., 11 Community Centre, Panchsheel Park,
New Delhi – 110 017, India
Penguin Group (NZ), cnr Airborne and Rosedale Roads, Albany,
Auckland 1310, New Zealand (a division of Pearson New Zealand Ltd.)
Penguin Books (South Africa) (Pty.) Ltd., 24 Sturdee Avenue,
Rosebank, Johannesburg 2196, South Africa

Penguin Books Ltd., Registered Offices:
80 Strand, London WC2R 0RL, England

First published by New American Library,
a division of Penguin Group (USA) Inc.

First Printing, February 2005
10 9 8 7 6 5 4 3 2 1

NEW AMERICAN LIBRARY and logo are trademarks of Penguin Group (USA) Inc.

LIBRARY OF CONGRESS CATALOGING-IN-PUBLICATION DATA:

Erotic love poems of Greece and Rome / translated by Stephen Bertman.
p. cm.
ISBN 0-451-21480-3 (Trade paperback)
1. Erotic poetry, Greek—Translations into English. 2. Love poetry, Classical—Translations into
English. 3. Erotic poetry, Latin—Translations into English. 4. Classical poetry—Translations into English.
I. Bertman, Stephen.
PA3624.E75E755 2005
880—dc22   2004016740

Set in Adobe Garamond
Designed by Ginger Legato

Printed in the United States of America

With love
to Elaine
(PROVERBS 31.10–31)

CONTENTS

INTRODUCTION

Erotic desire is as old as the human race, and erotic literature as old as civilization. Painted on fragile papyri disinterred from Egypt's sands and imprinted on clay tablets unearthed from Mesopotamia's wastes are the world's oldest love poems, dating back 3,500 years and more. These records testify not only to erotic passion but also to the impulse to articulate that passion in written form.

> *I am your first love, I am your garden,*
> *scented with spices, fragrant with flowers.*
> *Deep runs my channel, smoothed by your tillage,*
> *cooled by the North Wind, filled by the Nile.**

So wrote an Egyptian scribe in ancient days, even as a Mesopotamian poet wrote the words that follow:

> *Squeeze yourself into me*
> *as the hand presses flour*
> *into an open cup.*
> *Pound yourself into me*
> *as the fist rams flour into*
> *a cup craving to be filled.***

Such poems teach us that erotic passion has been an intrinsic component of human nature from civilization's beginnings.

Yet while love is spontaneous and free, poetry is by definition formal and structurally disciplined. While passion is personal and individualistic, literature is bound by tradition and convention. Love and passion

---

*Translated by Stephen Bertman. From Stephen Bertman, *Doorways Through Time: The Romance of Archaeology* (Los Angeles and New York: Tarcher/Putnam, 1986).
**Translated by Stephen Bertman. From Stephen Bertman, *Handbook to Life in Ancient Mesopotamia* (New York: Facts On File, 2003).

are natural and driven by emotion; literature and poetry, artificial and constrained by reason. How then can we account for the paradoxical marriage of love and poetry, for this age-old wedding of opposites?

First and foremost, love poems are expressions of feelings, but feelings can be chaotic unless they are given form. Such form endows feelings with a structure and compression they would otherwise lack. Their structure makes them more intelligible; their compression lends them power.

If a poem, then, is like a well-wrapped package, to whom is it sent? Surely, to the person the poet loves (or has come to hate); to other sympathetic listeners if the object of the poet's desire will not accept delivery; or even to the poet himself in order to make life more livable by externalizing frustration and the pain of rejection through the vehicle of the written word. Indeed, through the very act of literary composition, the poet can compose emotions, and in the process gain rational perspective and a renewed sense of erotic direction. The writing of poetry can thus help a poet's world make more sense, or at least make it bearable.

As a thing of beauty, a poem may also celebrate erotic pleasure found, lost, or longed for. Here form becomes the servant of art, transmuting otherwise ordinary words into noble statements, and bestowing the possibility of permanence on what might otherwise be only transitory and forgotten. It is sculpted form, not inchoate feeling, that gives ultimate satisfaction to poets, and it is form as much as content that has enabled their ancient poems to transcend the millennia and reach our own day, granting them an immortality that life itself withheld. As the biblical Song of Songs declares: "Love is as strong as death"—or at least, we may add, as long as love is enshrined in verse.

Yet if love poetry took root at civilization's inception, it did not flower until many centuries later. This is in large part due to the evolution of literacy itself. Though writing was invented in the ancient Near East, the types of writing that developed there—hieroglyphic and cuneiform—were highly complex systems consisting of hundreds upon hundreds of separate characters. Communication through writing thus became the prerogative of the learned few, and the written word was largely reserved for the formal prayers and archives of temple and palace, propagandistic inscriptions, and the calculating records of merchants. Composing love poetry, and reading it, would have been a leisure activity limited to a highly educated and numerically small elite. Indeed, even the political structure of Egyptian and Mesopotamian society conspired against the popularity of love poetry, since the individual and the aspirations of the individual were regarded as subservient to the theocratic state.

For erotic poetry to flower, what was needed was the democratization of love: an ideological environment that celebrated the individual and a simplified writing system that enabled such individuals to transcribe and read the personal messages of the human heart. This very environment arose for the first time not in the Near East but in Greece in the seventh century B.C.E., and its instrument was the alphabet, a Phoenician invention that the Greeks imported and adapted to their own humanistic, rather than theocratic, purposes. In Greek history the period is called the Archaic, but it is a misnomer, for the period was anything but old-fashioned as the name implies. The Archaic Period (about 750–490 B.C.E.) was an era of spiritual awakening as Greece emerged from four centuries of dark-age chaos that had followed the fall of the Heroic Age. The Archaic Period was a vibrant era of commercial expansionism, political revolution, and geographical exploration that witnessed the growth of independent city-states, the creation of the first life-size statues of Greek men and women, and the birth of personal poetry.

While Homeric epic had looked backward to glorious bygone days, Greek personal poetry focused on the promise of the present. While Homeric bards had suppressed their own personalities in commemorating the dead, the poets of the Archaic Period proclaimed the vivid uniqueness of their own identities. Epic poems might employ thousands of verses to convey scope and grandeur, but a personal poem could use ten or twenty lines and capture the essence of a moment. And while epic verse advanced with stately regularity, like wave after mighty wave rolling onto a sea's shore, personal poets invented variegated rhythms that glistened like crests on the breeze-tossed surface of a sunlit lake. To be sure, erotic motivation had always been interwoven with martial themes in Greek epic, but now eroticism came into its own as poetry's subject par excellence. At first came elegiac poetry, written conservatively in couplets and accompanied in performance by the flute; soon after came lyric poetry, more inventive in form and accompanied by the lyre.

The composition of personal poems, however, was eventually eclipsed by the rise of Greek patriotism. By the early fifth century B.C.E., after the Greeks had repelled two foreign invasions, Athens arose to become the country's richest and most powerful city-state and the home of a "Golden Age." The success of Athenian democracy in turn inspired celebratory literary genres that were communal rather than individualistic: history, oratory, and choral drama.

The rise of Athens, however, was followed within decades by its fall, as its imperialistic ambitions within Greece provoked a disastrous twenty-five-year-long war with Sparta, which ended in 404 B.C.E. with Athens' defeat. In the political and moral vacuum that followed, communalism withered and was replaced by a new emphasis on the individual. The failure of political idealism led, moreover, to a new stress on sensualism as the basis for personal happiness. The combined influence of individualism and sensualism, in turn, resulted in a renewed interest in erotic poetry, a trend that continued into the alternatingly exhilarating and confusing era known as the Hellenistic, initiated by the worldwide conquests of Alexander the Great.

With Alexander's death in 323 B.C.E., his empire fragmented. By the second century B.C.E., a new power arose, the power of Rome, an imperialistically ambitious state that by 146 B.C.E. became the political and military master of the Mediterranean world, including Greece. Though powerful, the Romans were by Greek standards crude and uneducated, a deficit the Romans had to make up if they were to command the cultural respect of the peoples they now ruled. Ever the pragmatists, the

Romans set about reinventing themselves by schooling themselves in all things Greek—all things, that is, that could be adapted to Roman taste and bent to Roman political purposes. Greek architecture (to express the bigness of Roman dreams), Greek sculpture (to express through portraiture and historical relief the bigness of the Roman ego), and Greek literature (especially history, epic, and oratory to glorify Roman achievements) fitted the bill very nicely.

About erotic poetry the macho Romans were a bit ambivalent. To some, it seemed too soft and unmanly to go on and on about love; indeed to many, writing poetry that was not overtly nationalistic or moralistic smacked of subversive effeminacy. But to talented others, the appeal was irresistible: to match the Greeks, or even outplay them, at their own literary game, and what a game it was! Power had always enticed the Romans, and the battle of the sexes was the ultimate arena, far more intoxicating and pleasurable than fighting the barbarians. If the Greek poet had fixated on the evanescence of life and the fragility of beauty, the Roman poet would extol the mastery (albeit temporary) of man over woman. Of course, who was the slave and who was the master would remain the eternal question. Thanks to the written word, some Roman poets even immortalized their mistresses, though it could be argued that it was their mistresses who in the end immortalized them!

The great age of Roman erotic poetry was the late Republic and nascent Empire, especially the age of Augustus Caesar (27 B.C.E.–14 C.E.), the so-called "Golden Age of Rome," a time of imperialistic affluence enjoyed by a sensually liberated class of rich and leisured patricians. Though later decades became more corrupt—the so-called days of "bread and circuses"—for some reason the writing and reading of erotic poetry was to wane, perhaps because the Romans became more interested in "doing it" than in describing it, or perhaps because moral corruption so debases the possibilities of heartfelt art that such art ceases to be created.

Ironically though, erotic poetry *did* continue to be written, not in the western but in the eastern Mediterranean, and not in Latin but in Greek, well into the Byzantine Period. The embers of love do not so readily die, nor does the capacity of love to inspire passionate poetry.

THE CHALLENGE OF TRANSLATION

> It was already one in the morning; the rain pattered dismally against the panes, and my candle was nearly burnt out, when, by the glimmer of the half-extinguished light, I saw the dull yellow eye of the creature open; it breathed hard, and a convulsive motion agitated its limbs.

With these words, Victor Frankenstein described with trembling recollection the birth of his creature. The words are recorded in Mary Shelley's 1818 novel, *Frankenstein*. Yet in the memorable film adaptation of 1931, he utters words even more dramatic, crying out as the creature opens its eyes, "It's alive! It's alive!"

They are words that every prospective translator, especially a translator of ancient poetry, should take to heart, for unless the poem in its new linguistic incarnation lives and breathes as an organic whole, it is no more than a mechanical assemblage of bodily parts "collected . . . from charnel-houses and disturbed, with profane fingers . . ."

Of course, it is no easy task to take something long dead and give it life. To do so, the prospective translator must first rationally assess, as well as one can, the literal meaning of the dead poet's words through diligent recourse to dictionaries, grammars, and scholarly commentaries. But having once established that literal meaning, he or she must then attempt to spiritually "inhabit" the poem, repeatedly reflecting on that meaning, reading the poem again and again in its original language, and persistently searching for an emotional key by which the world of the poem can be unlocked. In the end, that key will prove a personal one, as personal for the translator as it was for the original poet. And while it might seem useful in such an enterprise to familiarize oneself with the poet's life—and surely it is—we must at the same time humbly acknowledge that most of what we will know about an ancient poet's life will paradoxically derive from our understanding of the poems themselves.

Yet assuming the translator has emotionally entered an erotic poem, how does he or she then effectively exit? For if we are to be more successful than mythical Orpheus, we must not only venture into the land of the dead but, to validate our efforts, return from it with a Eurydice we can hold in our arms. Our "Eurydice" will need to be not a bloodless avatar but, as nearly as is possible, a spiritually authentic equivalent of the original work, warm and pulsing with life.

That is no simple matter, however. Words in one language, though they may be equivalent in meaning to words in another, may be dissimilar in color or cadence; at other times, more words may be needed in one language to communicate what can be said in another with fewer. Furthermore, the versification of both ancient Greek and Latin poetry depends on abstract rhythms, or meters, based on intricate combinations of short and long syllables (short = one beat; long = two), a characteristic almost impossible to replicate for long stretches in English. Indeed, it is these formal patterns that give Classical poems their artistic structure, that make them "poems." Traditional English poetry, on the other hand, is marked by end rhyme (". . . moon" / ". . . June"), a feature virtually absent from Classical verse. Last, ancient Greek, a musical language, used rising-and-falling tonal accents (like Chinese), not softer-or-louder stress accents like English (or, for that matter, like Latin).

Literal meaning aside, how then do we convert a Greek or Latin poem into an English one when there are so many structural differences? The honest answer is: with great difficulty. The art of translation can be compared to a process of negotiation, one in which trade-offs are grudgingly made by labor or management to save an endangered company's life. Only in this case, it is not a company's life but a poet's, a poet who is counting on us to do him or her justice. Such trade-offs may require the translator to use rhyme where rhythm alone will not impress, or substitute one rhythm for another that works better in English, or at times update an archaic image to ensure the poem will retain the impact the author intended. Or sometimes, painfully, to leave something out because its inclusion in English would interrupt the flow of language. Close at hand, the translator must also have a trusty thesaurus (to help him find just the right word) and, at times, a rhyming dictionary.

Inevitably, as Victor Frankenstein found out, the stitches may show. But if the translator has done his work honestly and well, and has shown his creature both love and compassion (as the creator in the novel did not), then that creature will *not* turn out to be a monster. And when the translator proclaims, "It's alive! It's alive!" he will be able to do so with justifiable pride and share his victory with others.

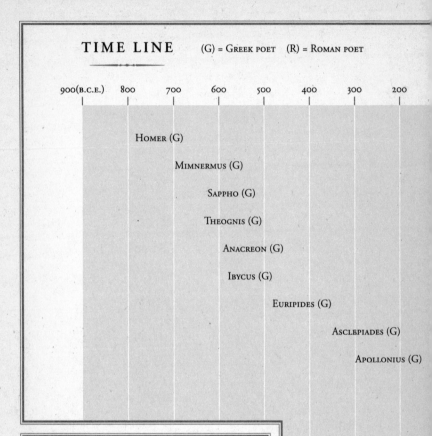

TIME LINE (G) = Greek poet (R) = Roman poet

900(b.c.e.)	800	700	600	500	400	300	200

Homer (G)

Mimnermus (G)

Sappho (G)

Theognis (G)

Anacreon (G)

Ibycus (G)

Euripides (G)

Asclepiades (G)

Apollonius (G)

Historical Periods and Events

Heroic Age of Greece: 15th–13th centuries b.c.e

Fall of Troy: 13th century b.c.e

Dark Ages of Greece: 12/11th–8th centuries b.c.e

Archaic Period: 8th–6th centuries b.c.e

Golden Age of Athens: 5th century b.c.e

Beginning of the Hellenistic Age: 4th century b.c.e

Roman Republic: 509–27 b.c.e

Roman Empire: 27 b.c.e–476 c.e (Fall of Rome)

Golden Age of Rome (Augustan Age): 27 b.c.e–14 c.e

200	100	I/I(C.E.)	100	200	300	400	500	600

MOSCHUS (G)

BION (G) AND THE ALEXANDRIAN EROTIC FRAGMENT (G)

MELEAGER (G)

PHILODEMUS (G)

ANTIPATER OF THESSALONICA (G)

MARCUS ARGENTARIUS (G)

STRATO (G)

RUFINUS (G)

PAULUS
SILENTARIUS (G)

CATULLUS (R)

VERGIL (R)

HORACE (R)

TIBULLUS (R)

SULPICIA (R)

PROPERTIUS (R)

OVID (R)

MARTIAL (R)

THE PERVIGILIUM VENERIS (R)

Erotic Love Poems
of
GREECE
AND
ROME

Erotic Love Poems

of

Greece

HOMER

(EIGHTH CENTURY B.C.E.)

Among the names of Western civilization's authors, Homer's is the oldest we possess, though the poet's exact identity is a matter of scholarly conjecture. What is beyond debate, however, is that Homer was a master storyteller who gave consummate poetic expression to traditional heroic tales and cast them in a dramatic form they would forever retain. Homer's inspiration was the Trojan War (thirteenth century B.C.E.), an epic conflict that left an everlasting impression on Greek memory and imagination. Homer's poems, *The Iliad* and *The Odyssey*, recounted the story of that war and its aftermath.

Yet the world of Homeric epic is not purely martial, for love pervades it. The Trojan War was itself instigated by an act of sexual passion: the abduction of Helen, whose face "launched a thousand ships," a femme fatale who would later live on in romantic memory as Helen "of Troy." And, despite the allure of divine enchantresses and the savagery of bloodthirsty monsters, it was the image of faithful and beloved Penelope that guided Odysseus as he struggled for years against wind and wave to return home.

In addition to *The Iliad* and *The Odyssey*, we also possess other poems composed in the same epic style: hymns to the gods and brief epigrams that are attributed to Homer and his fellow bards.

APHRODITE DIRECTS A LOVE SCENE (THE ILIAD, 3:380–447)

The most famous war in Greek memory, the Trojan War, was provoked by an act of seduction and adultery. With the collusion of Aphrodite, the Greek goddess of sex, Alexander (also known as Paris) ran off with a married woman named

Helen. Alexander was a dashingly handsome bachelor prince from the royal house of Troy, a city on the coast of present-day Turkey; Helen, renowned as the most beautiful woman of her day, was married to Menelaus, king of the Greek city of Sparta. To retrieve Helen, the Greeks laid siege to Troy, waging war for a decade until Troy finally fell. During the long conflict, Helen became filled with self-loathing: out of momentary passion she had renounced her homeland, her husband, and her child only to become an object of whispered derision among foreigners upon whom she had brought the curse of war. Yet she and her lover, Alexander, were still drawn to each other and were still Aphrodite's playthings. As our scene opens, Aphrodite rescues Alexander from the plain before Troy where he was engaged in a duel with Menelaus, a duel that Helen had been watching from Troy's battlements.

. . . Aphrodite rescued Alexander—no hard job
for a goddess—by wrapping him in thick mist.
She set him down in a bedroom fragrant with incense,
and then went off to summon Helen.
She found her standing on the city wall, surrounded by the women
    of Troy.
Taking hold of Helen's scented robe with her hand, the goddess
    tugged at it,
and spoke to her disguised as an old crone,
a woman who used to card fine wool for Helen
when they lived in Sparta, a servant Helen used to like.
Disguised in this way, divine Aphrodite spoke to her and said:
"Come along now. Alexander is calling for you to come home.
The man's in his bedroom lying on that ornate bed,
so handsome and handsomely dressed you wouldn't think
he'd just come from a battlefield, but instead was going
to a dance, or was just sitting down after dancing."

So she spoke, and stirred up desire in Helen's heart.
But when Helen recognized the goddess' lovely neck,
the beautiful breasts, and sparkling eyes,
she was taken aback and addressed her:
"Goddess, why do you want to deceive me this way?
Is it your plan now to lure me to some big city
—in Phrygia perhaps or scenic Maionia—
assuming there's a male there you fancy—
now that Menelaus has beaten Alexander
and intends to drag me back home?
Is that why you're standing here scheming?
Go sit by him yourself then. Give up your godly ways
and forget the road back to Olympus.
Why don't *you* watch over and cry over him
until he makes you his wife or, maybe, his slave?
Don't count on me to go and shamefully
share that man's bed. All the women of Troy
would chastise me if I did, and I have enough trouble already!"
Incensed, divine Aphrodite spoke out:
"Don't provoke me, bitch, or I'll get even and desert you,
and hate you as much as I've loved you up until now.
I'll put you right in the middle and make both sides despise you,
Trojans and Greeks alike, so you'll meet an awful end."
So she spoke, and Helen, child of Zeus, trembled.
Covering herself up in a radiant wrap, she went on her way
in silence, evading the Trojan women's notice, the goddess leading
    the way.
Now when they arrived at Alexander's splendid residence,
the serving women quickly busied themselves with their tasks,
while godlike Helen made her way to his high-ceilinged chamber.
Laughter-loving Aphrodite took hold of a bench
and, carrying it, set it in front of Alexander.
Helen, daughter of aegis-bearing Zeus, sat down on it
and, turning her eyes away from her lover, reproached him:

"So you've returned then from battle. Perhaps you should have died
     there,
vanquished by the valiant man who used to be my husband.
Once you boasted you were a better man than Ares' darling, Menelaus,
whether fighting with your bare hands or your spear.
So why don't you now challenge Ares' darling, Menelaus,
and fight once again face-to-face? If I could only have my way
I'd beg you to stop, and forget fair-haired Menelaus
and all this warfare and foolish fighting
for fear you'll someday soon fall to his spear."
Paris then responded to her, saying:
"Don't criticize me, woman, with such harsh words.
Menelaus may have just beaten me with Athena's help,
but I'll beat him someday. After all, I have gods on my side too!
But come on, let's go to bed and enjoy ourselves by making love.
Never before have I felt passion like this sweep over my senses,
not even when I sailed away from lovely Lacedaemon,
after taking you on board my seagoing ship,
and on the island of Cranae first made love to you in bed.
I long for you now the same way, and am overwhelmed by sweet desire."
He spoke, and led the way to bed, and his lover followed along.

Though desire, as Paris states, can be sweet, this excerpt
from *The Iliad* shows it can also be cruel. Mythology makes
Aphrodite the mother of Eros, or Cupid, but to the Greeks
she was not a manufacturer of lacy Valentine's Day cards. In
Greek her name meant "foam-born" because of the story
that she had arisen from the seminal foam that had floated
on the sea after the primal god Cronus castrated his father,
Uranus, and threw his severed genitals into the waves. Born
of such an act of sexual violence, Aphrodite could herself be
savage, bestowing her sensual blessings on humans while at
the same time bending them mercilessly to her implacable
will. As Helen learns, she is no deity to be trifled with. The

poet invokes Aphrodite's nature by playing on our senses (a fragrant bedroom, a scented robe, a lovely neck), while at the same time costuming the goddess as a postmenopausal crone for contrast. Of course, Aphrodite still lives today in the hormones that surge through our bloodstreams, inciting in us a desire for erotic gratification that can be—as it was for Helen—mindless of all consequence.

ANDROMACHE BEGS HER HUSBAND TO "MAKE LOVE NOT WAR"
(THE ILIAD, 6:392–496)

Hector was the bravest warrior the Trojans had. Governing his life was a heroic code that demanded he defend his people even at the price of his own life. To do less would be to suffer shame and dishonor in the eyes of his countrymen. The war has raged on now for nine years and Hector knows Troy's cause is lost, yet his conduct is still bound by the same mortal rules. In the following passage, his wife, Andromache, pleads with him not to go out and fight again.

As he crossed the great city and came to the gate,
the Scaean Gate, through which he meant to exit to the plain,
his treasured wife came running up to him,
Andromache, daughter of proud-hearted Eëtion,
Eëtion, who lived beneath woody Mount Placus,
in Placan Thebe, as lord of the Cilicians.
It was his daughter who now clung to helmeted Hector.
She had gone to meet him there along with her maidservant
who in her bosom was holding an innocent child, just an infant,
Hector's beloved son, bright as a star,
a boy he had named Scamandrius (after the city's river), but others
called Astyanax ("Lord of the City"), because Hector was its chief
    defense.
Casting a silent glance at the child, he smiled,
but, standing beside her husband, Andromache began to cry,

and, taking his hand in hers, spoke to him and said:
"Husband, your courage will kill you. Have you no pity
for your infant son or your poor wife who is to become
your widow? The Achaeans are going to kill you soon
when they all attack. As for me, I'd rather
go to my grave if it means losing you, because I won't have
any comfort when you meet your fate,
just grief. I don't have a father or a queenly mother,
for godlike Achilles slew my father
when he destroyed the populous city of the Cilicians,
Thebe of the lofty gates. He took Eëtion's life
yet didn't strip the armor from his body, for he had scruples,
and instead burned him together with his well-wrought gear,
piling a mound over him around which elm trees were planted
by the mountain nymphs, daughters of aegis-bearing Zeus.
I had seven brothers in the palace
and all went to Hades on the selfsame day,
for swift-footed, godlike Achilles slaughtered them
within sight of their ambling cattle and white-fleeced sheep.
As for my mother, who ruled as queen beneath woody Placus,
when Achilles brought her here with everything she owned,
he set her free in exchange for a rich ransom,
but later she died in her father's palace, struck by Artemis' arrow.
For all these reasons, Hector, *you* are my father and my mother
and my brother too, besides being the lover who shares my bed.
Take pity and stay here behind the wall.
Don't make your son an orphan and your wife a widow.
Station the army at the wild fig tree, where the city is most
vulnerable and the wall can be most readily scaled.
Three times already the Greeks have tried to enter there
—the two Ajaxes and illustrious Idomeneus
along with the sons of Atreus and Tydeus' mighty son—
either because some shrewd seer gave them advice
or their own instincts showed them the way and led them on."

Then Hector of the shimmering helmet answered her:
"These things, wife, prey on my mind too, but I worry over
what the Trojan men and their long-robed women might think
if I showed myself a coward and refrained from war.
My character likewise resists, for I was always taught to be brave
and fight in the front line beside my comrades
to gain glory for my father and myself.
I well realize in my heart and soul
that the day is coming when holy Troy will fall
together with Priam of the ashen spear and Priam's people.
But the anguish I feel is mostly not for what lies ahead for Troy,
or for Queen Hecuba or King Priam themselves,
or for my brothers, many and brave,
who will fall in the dust at the hands of the enemy,
but for *you*, when some of the bronze-clad Achaeans
lead you away weeping after they rob you of your freedom;
when, in Argos, you ply someone else's loom
and fetch water from Messeis or Hypereia
against your will when harsh necessity compels;
or when someone says, seeing you shed a tear,
'That's the wife of Hector over there, who of all the horse-taming
    Trojans
shone when our warriors fought around Troy.'
So someone may say. And fresh sorrow will consume you,
knowing you lack such a man to bring your slavery to an end.
May my corpse be buried beneath the earth
before I hear you cry as they carry you away."
Having said these words, glorious Hector stretched out his arms to
    hold his son,
but the child pulled back and, bawling, buried his head in his nurse's
    bosom,
frightened at his father's appearance:
the bronze face, and the horsehair crest
that shook from his helmet's top.

At this, his beloved father and mother both broke into laughter,
and Hector immediately removed the helmet from his head
and set it down on the ground, where it shimmered in the light.
Kissing his dear son and lifting him up in his arms,
he raised a prayer to Zeus and the other gods:
"Zeus and you other gods, grant that this son of mine
may be, like his father, a man of distinction in Troy,
valiant and brave, a mighty ruler of the Trojans.
And one day may someone say, as my son returns from battle,
'There goes a man even better than his father!' And as he carries
    home the armor
of the enemy he has slain, may his mother's heart be glad."
Having so spoken, he put his son in his dear wife's arms,
and she pressed him into her fragrant bosom,
smiling through tears. Noticing this, her husband took pity on her,
and touched her face with his hand and said:
"Wife, don't trouble your heart over me too much.
No one can send me to Hades unless it's my destiny,
and no mortal can escape his fate,
coward or hero, once he is born.
But go home now and take care of your housework,
the loom and the distaff, and tell the maidservants
to go about their tasks. Let war be the business of men,
of all men, especially me, who live in Troy."

In this poignant intermission from combat, the poet Homer
allows us to view war through the eyes of a soldier's helpless
wife. Yet her strong arguments in the name of love and com-
mitment inevitably fail, and she is impotent to stop her hus-
band from returning to a war in which he will soon die.
Tragically, Hector is as impotent as she: trained in a heroic
code that will allow no breach, and constrained by commu-
nal pressure, he must fight to the death in a losing cause
with grim fatalism as his only consolation. To Homer's audi-

ence, the irony ran deeper. Besides knowing that Hector would later die and that Andromache would be made an enemy's concubine, they knew Hector's prayer would be in vain: in the end when Troy fell, the infant Astyanax would be hurled to his death from Troy's battlements by the savage victors. It is that baby—humorously brought to tears by the sight of a helmet—who most humanizes the scene while prefiguring its tragic outcome.

CALYPSO SAYS FAREWELL TO ODYSSEUS (THE ODYSSEY, 5:192–227)

After the Trojan war, the beautiful but lonely goddess Calypso held the shipwrecked hero Odysseus prisoner on her remote island, offering him the gift of immortality if only he would agree to stay with her and be her lover for all eternity. Yearning to return home to his family and kingdom, where he was desperately needed, Odysseus steadfastly refused her offer, even though his refusal would ultimately mean his death and an afterlife to be spent in the dreariness of Hades' ghostly realm. Now orders from Mount Olympus, brought by the messenger god Hermes, have directed Calypso to release Odysseus from captivity. Though unwilling, she must obey.

Having so spoken, the divine goddess quickly
led the way, and he followed in the goddess' footsteps,
and the two—goddess and man—came to the hollow cave.
For his part, he took a seat on the chair where Hermes
had only recently sat, and the nymph laid out all sorts of things
for him to eat and drink, the sustenance consumed by mortals.
For her part, she sat down opposite godlike Odysseus,
while her attendants placed ambrosia and nectar before her.
Both then partook of the refreshments set before them.
But when they were satisfied with eating and drinking,
the divine goddess Calypso began to speak.

"Heavenly born son of Laertes, cunning Odysseus,
do you really want to go straight home now to your
beloved homeland? Well then, good luck to you!
Yet if you truly knew how many troubles
fate had in store for you before you arrived,
you'd stay here at home with me
and become immortal, in spite of the longing you feel
for that wife you keep dreaming of every day.
Surely you can't claim I'm inferior to her
in looks or stature, since in no way can mortals
rival the gods in appearance."
In response, cunning Odysseus replied:
"Revered goddess, do not be angry with me over this.
I readily acknowledge that—compared to you—
prudent Penelope is no match in stature or looks,
for she is mortal, while you are immortal and ageless.
But nevertheless I long every day to go home
and experience the moment of my return.
And should some god smash me with his fist on the wine-dark deep,
I shall endure the pain, for my heart well knows affliction,
having long suffered and striven on battlefield and sea.
I shall merely add that to all the rest I have known."
So he spoke, and the sun set and darkness came on.
Then the two of them walked to the innermost part of the hollow
    cave,
and took pleasure in making love, lying in each other's arms.

In this description of leave-taking, the poet contrasts two in-
compatible worlds. Endowed with human emotions, the
Greek gods had human appetites, including sexual hunger.
But these appetites were doomed to be frustrated, some-
times tragically, if the objects of their passion were human
and had peculiarly human needs. Thus the mortal hero re-
jects the love-starved goddess because everlasting life on

her remote island would require his rejection of those things, however imperfect and evanescent, that would give his life its deepest meaning. In the end, across that metaphysical divide, the two lovers embrace before they are to part forever.

THE ADULTEROUS LOVE AFFAIR OF ARES AND APHRODITE
(THE ODYSSEY, 8:266–366)

On his journey home from Calypso's island, Odysseus was shipwrecked on the Phaeacian coast. Received by the royal family in their palace, Odysseus was welcomed and shown hospitality. During the feast, a court minstrel sings of an adulterous sexual liaison between two gods: Ares, the Greek god of war, and Aphrodite, the goddess of sexual attraction and the wife of the blacksmith god, Hephaestus.

Strumming his lyre, the minstrel lifted up his voice in song, singing of the love affair of Ares and diademed Aphrodite,
how they first had intercourse in Hephaestus' house
in secret and how Ares, after giving her many gifts, dishonored the bed
of lord Hephaestus. Helios, the god of the sun, had reported it to her husband
after spying the two lying together and making love.
Now as soon as Hephaestus heard the disturbing news,
he went to his smithy to formulate a plan of revenge.
Setting his mighty anvil on the anvil block, he forged fetters
that could not be broken or undone in order to hold the lovers tight.
He fashioned the snare, inspired by his anger at Ares,
and then made his way to the chamber where the bed lay.
Wrapping the fetters round and round the bedposts,
he hung others down from the rafters
fine as spiderwebs so no one could see,
not even the blessed gods, so cunningly were they fashioned.
And when the whole trap was laid about the bed,
he made a show of going to the well-built citadel of Lemnos,

which of all lands was the one closest to his heart.
Golden-reined Ares, ever on the lookout, didn't fail
to notice talented Hephaestus setting out on his trip.
So Ares made his way to the renowned god's house,
eager to make love again to diademed Aphrodite.
She had just returned from a visit to her mighty father, Zeus,
and was seated as Ares entered the house.
Taking her hand in his, he spoke her name, saying:
"Come, my love, let's go to bed and enjoy ourselves there.
Hephaestus is no longer around, for he's gone to Lemnos
to pay a call on the savage-tongued Sintians."
So he spoke, and she welcomed his invitation to go to bed.
But as the two of them entered the bedroom and lay down,
the fetters fashioned by clever Hephaestus instantly wrapped around
    them,
making it impossible for them to move their limbs or get up.
It was then they realized there would be no escape.
Meanwhile, the famous crippled god was approaching.
Before ever reaching Lemnos, he had turned back,
prompted by Helios, who was keeping watch for him.
So Hephaestus made his way back home with a heavy heart.
And now as he stood in the doorway, he was overcome with rage
and uttered a terrible cry, calling out to all the gods.
"Father Zeus and you other blessed gods who live forever,
come here and witness a cruel joke:
because I'm lame, Zeus' daughter Aphrodite
perpetually dishonors me, choosing instead now to love Ares the
    destroyer,
because he's handsome and sound of foot compared to me,
who was born disfigured. For that I can only blame
my two parents, who never should have given me birth.
But come and see the very bed, my bed, where they lay down
to make love, a sight that even now pains my eyes to see.
I don't think they'll want to lie this way much longer,

even though they're very much in love. Soon enough they'll
lose their desire to sleep together. Even so the trap will hold them tight
until her father gives me back all the presents
I put in his hands for the sake of that shameless daughter of his,
shameless because she's beautiful but can't control her emotions."
So he spoke, and the gods assembled at his bronze-paved house.
Poseidon the Earth-shaker, Hermes the Luck-bringer, and Apollo the
    Archer-god all came,
but the tender goddesses stayed home out of embarrassment.
Givers of blessings, the male gods stood in the doorway,
and unquenchable laughter arose among them
when they beheld how crafty clever Hephaestus had been.
Glancing at his neighbor, one said to the other:
"Crime doesn't pay. The slow can catch the quick.
See how Hephaestus, sluggish as he is, caught Ares,
the fastest of the gods who dwell on Olympus.
Hephaestus may be lame on foot, but his mind is nimble,
and Ares owes him the adulterer's fine."
This is the kind of thing one god said to the other.
Then Lord Apollo, Zeus' son, spoke to Hermes:
"Hermes, son of Zeus, guide and giver of blessings,
would you be willing to be held in the grip of such a snare
if you could lie in bed with golden Aphrodite?"
And the guide and slayer of Argus replied:
"That would be my desire, Lord Apollo, Archer-god!
In fact, I'd be glad to have three times as many fetters holding me fast
with all of you gods and goddesses watching,
if only I could lie next to golden Aphrodite!"
So he spoke, and the immortal gods broke out in laughter.
But Poseidon wasn't laughing. Instead he kept begging
Hephaestus, famous for his handiwork, to release Ares,
and addressed Hephaestus with winged words:
"Let him go. I promise that, just as you ask,
he'll pay the whole fine in front of the immortal gods."

Then the famous crippled god replied:
"Don't ask me to do this, Earth-shaker Poseidon.
The debts of worthless people aren't worth betting on.
How could I ever hold you responsible before the immortal gods
if Ares escapes his fetters *and* his debts?"
To that Earth-shaker Poseidon replied:
"Hephaestus, even if Ares goes and runs away
to avoid paying his fine, I myself will pay whatever he owes."
Then the famous crippled god replied:
"How can I then possibly refuse you?"
So saying, mighty Hephaestus unloosed the fetters
and the two lovers, freed from those strong restraints,
leaped out of bed—Ares taking off for Thrace
and laughter-loving Aphrodite for Paphos
in Cyprus, where her sacred temple and fragrant altar lie.
There the Graces bathed her and anointed her with immortal
oil, the sort that covers the gods who live forever,
clothed her in lovely raiment, and made her a wonder to behold.

Though the gods and goddesses of the Greeks lived on
the heights of Mount Olympus, their impulses and behavior
could be earthy indeed. Unlike the deity of the Bible, Greek
divinities were not symbols of a morality higher than that of
common humanity: Greek gods could bear false witness,
murder, covet, and—as we have seen—commit adultery.
Though the Greeks themselves revered their gods because
they were forced to acknowledge heaven's awesome pow-
ers, they could also—as here—make them the butt of hu-
mor. As has been often said, unlike the God of the Bible,
who created man in His own image, the humanistic Greeks
created their gods as reflections of their own human quali-
ties, including their folly and foibles. There is also a dramatic
subtext to our passage. Coming as it does in *The Odyssey*
before Odysseus' return home to his wife, Penelope, the

theme of the minstrel's song is meant to suggest a hidden anxiety Odysseus may harbor over the issue of his wife's sexual fidelity during their twenty-year separation. As Homer is to later say (*The Odyssey*, 17:36–37), "Prudent Penelope came from her chamber looking like Artemis or golden Aphrodite." The key word is "or." During Odysseus' absence, had she been more like chaste Artemis or lustful Aphrodite? For the returning hero, only time would tell. Unlike Hephaestus, he couldn't depend on the watchful eye of a Helios to tell him. Besides, he had been guilty of his own sexual indiscretions, having slept with goddesses—though, according to an ancient Greek double standard, he was granted heroic exemption from blame.

ODYSSEUS AND HIS WIFE, PENELOPE, ARE REUNITED
(THE ODYSSEY, 23:205–46)

When the hero Odysseus finally returned home and killed the arrogant suitors who had occupied his palace, he might have expected his wife, Penelope, to welcome him with open arms. But Penelope was as wily as her husband. Suspecting that her "deliverer" might in fact be a pretender, she decided to test him. When they had first married, Odysseus had built their bedroom around an olive tree that grew in the courtyard of their home. Leaving the tree rooted to the ground, he had carved their bedpost from its stout trunk. Now, twenty years later, Penelope slyly announces she will have the bed brought out so her newly arrived "husband" can get some rest. Mistakenly assuming that Penelope had sawn the bed from its roots, Odysseus becomes enraged, describes the way he had originally constructed their bed, and thereby proves his identity to his doubting wife.

So he spoke, and her knees and heart melted
as she recognized the proof Odysseus gave her.

Dissolving into tears, she ran straight toward him and threw her arms
around her husband's neck, kissed his head, and said:
"Don't be upset with me, Odysseus. I knew you would be smarter
than other men. It's the gods we should blame,
who jealously kept the two of us apart, preventing us
from together enjoying our youth and reaching the threshold of
    old age.
Don't be angry and resent me
because I didn't show you affection from the moment I first saw you,
for my heart trembled, afraid that some man might have come
to trick me, for there are many who use their wiles for wicked ends.
Born of Zeus, Argive Helen herself wouldn't have
slept in another man's bed had she known the consequences:
that the warlike sons of the Achaeans
would have dragged her back to her native land.
It was a god that inspired her to commit that shameful act
that she never would have contemplated on her own,
an act that would eventually cause you and me such heartache.
And now, because you've offered me such clear proof
by telling the story of our bed, a story no one else knows
except you and me and a single maid,
Actoris, whom Father gave me when I was a bride,
the maid who always used to shut our bedroom door tight,
you have convinced me, however much I may have seemed heartless
    before."
So she spoke and made him release the tears he was repressing,
and holding his perceptive and beloved wife in his arms, he wept.
Just as when the mainland is sighted by swimmers
whose well-built ship the sea god has smashed,
battering it with wind and massive waves,
so that a few, swimming to shore, escape the gray sea
and—though their bodies are caked with brine—
joyously step onto land, having outrun evil,
so to Penelope was her husband welcome as she beheld him,

nor was she able to release her white arms from around his neck.
And now rosy-fingered Dawn would have arisen to find them still
    weeping
had not the gray-eyed goddess Athena taken notice.
She held back Night at the western horizon and
detained golden-throned Dawn on the east, nor let
the swift-footed colts be yoked that bear light to mankind,
Lampus and Phaëthon, that draw the chariot of Dawn.

> In this emotional scene of reunion, the poet portrays hus-
> band and wife, Odysseus and Penelope, as mirror images of
> each other. Throughout *The Odyssey*, Homer had depicted
> Odysseus, the seafaring survivor, as a wily dissembler, wary
> and distrustful of others' motives; now in this episode, the
> poet depicts Penelope, a domestic survivor, in similar fashion.
> All along, Odysseus had been the perpetually shipwrecked
> hero, struggling to shore after shore, through wind and waves,
> ever seeking home; now, in a stunning reversal, the poet ap-
> plies the simile of the swimmer to Penelope, as Odysseus
> becomes the longed-for mainland that she at last can tear-
> fully embrace. Odysseus himself is not above crying. He had
> long wept on Calypso's isle, looking helplessly out to sea,
> and at last is home. The goddess Athena makes up for lost
> time by stopping time itself so the two can make love during
> the course of a divinely prolonged night.

A NAKED APHRODITE IS DRESSED
(THE SECOND HOMERIC HYMN TO APHRODITE)

August Aphrodite, crowned in gold and beauty,
I celebrate, whose dominion is the battlements of sea-girt
Cyprus, where the force of the moist West Wind
carried her across the crashing sea
in frothy foam. There the gold-ribboned Hours, welcoming her
with gladness, wrapped her round in divine raiment,

placing on her immortal head a finely wrought crown
beautiful and golden, and in her pierced earlobes
set flowers of natural brass and precious gold.
About her tender neck and silver-white breasts
they draped golden necklaces like the ones
they adorned themselves with whenever they attended
the elegant dances held by the gods in their father's home.
And when they had arrayed her body in every ornament,
they brought her to the immortals, who, as their eyes held her,
embraced her, each god praying that he might
lead her home to make her his wedded wife,
marveling at the sight of violet-crowned Cytheria.

In this brief hymn to the goddess of love, the poet describes how Aphrodite—newly born at sea in full-grown form—was bedecked by divine attendants for her heavenly debut. Far from dwelling on the goddess' naked sensuality, the hymn reverently describes her as a regal figure arrayed in queenly splendor whose beauty makes the male gods of heaven instantly desire her. On a wall painting that survives from the buried Roman city of Pompeii, we can see the goddess, wafted across the sea on a seashell, naked except for jewelry. The Italian Renaissance painter Botticelli in his *Birth of Venus* would later portray her completely naked except for what a modest pose and ample auburn hair could obscure.

A HUMAN LOVER UNDRESSES THE GODDESS OF LOVE
(THE FIRST HOMERIC HYMN TO APHRODITE, 5:155–67)

Zeus, the king of the Greek gods, resented the fact that Aphrodite had power over all the Olympians including himself, since Aphrodite could make anyone, even immortals, fall in love. He therefore decided to teach her a lesson by making her fall in love herself and become pregnant. The mate he selected for her was Anchises, a member of Troy's royal family.

So saying, he took her by the hand. And laughter-loving Aphrodite,
with her lovely eyes downcast, demurely approached
the hero's bed, which was spread with soft coverlets
on which he had laid the skins of bears and roaring lions
that he himself had slain in the high mountains.
And once they were on the bed,
Anchises first removed the bright ornaments from her body
—the brooches and armlets, the earrings and necklaces—
and, loosening her belt, slipped off her glistening garments
and set them down on a silver-studded chair.
Then by divine will and destiny
he, a mere mortal, lay with an immortal goddess, not fully realizing
   what he did.

The child Aphrodite would bear to Anchises would be named Aeneas. As a young man, Aeneas fought valiantly in the Trojan War. According to a legend elaborated upon in Vergil's *Aeneid*, after the fall of Troy, Aeneas led a band of Trojan refugees to Italy, where they helped propagate the Roman race.

A SENIOR CITIZEN'S PRAYER (HOMERIC EPIGRAMS, 12)
Hear my prayer, nursemaid of youth, and grant
that she may reject the seductive appeal of young men
and instead enjoy the company of men with graying temples
whose prime may be past but whose spirit is alive with longing.

In this four-verse prayer composed in epic style, the poet appeals for divine aid to attain his erotic objective. This is the earliest documentary evidence, but certainly not the last we will see in Classical literature, of a yearning by older poets for erotic gratification, and a frustration that their age makes them physically unappealing to the youthful objects of their desire. Perhaps significantly, the poet directs his prayer not to Aphrodite (who might have been more inclined to listen to those who were physically robust) but to Hecate, the "nursemaid of youth," a goddess to whom the men of his day prayed for success and whom Zeus had made a guardian of the young.

MIMNERMUS

According to tradition, Mimnermus of Colophon (a Greek colony on the west coast of Turkey), a piper as well as an elegiac poet, loved a fellow musician, a woman named Nanno. Only two of Mimnermus' elegies survive intact, both on the evanescence of youth. The rest of his poems are ironic proof of that evanescence since they endure only as fragments.

THE PRECIOUSNESS OF LOVE (1.1)

What kind of life, what kind of pleasure can exist without golden
    Aphrodite?
  May I die when these things no longer matter to me:
a flirtation in the dark, the gifts that sweethearts give, and bed—
    the blooms of youth that every man and woman
wants to pick. For when painful old age comes,
    disfiguring even a handsome man,
his mind becomes exhausted with care
    and his eyes no longer relish sunlight,
detested by boys, insulted by women.
    Such is the burden God has made of old age.

The Greeks, who loved beauty so passionately, were tortured by the realization that their souls were trapped within bodily prisons that became progressively more ugly with age, making the fulfillment of erotic desire less and less likely. Through the craft of poetry, such frustration might, as here, be transmuted into art. Mimnermus' poem is the first of many to come down from Classical antiquity that addressed such a theme. It is also the first to refer to Greek pedastry, the "love of boys."

SAPPHO

(SEVENTH–SIXTH CENTURY B.C.E.)

In the Classical world, writing was not a woman's occupation, and for Greek and Roman women, even literacy could be rare. It is all the more remarkable, then, that we have Sappho. Later called by Plato "the Tenth Muse" (mythology gave the Greeks only nine such divinities), she was the first poet in the world to devote herself exclusively to chronicling love. *Whom* she loved is the question later ages would ask. Was it men, women, or both? The fact that almost all of her poems survive in fragments—preserved by later writers or on scraps of crumbling papyrus, with some fragments only one word long—makes the job of reconstructing her work, let alone her private life, impossibly difficult. We know from tradition that she married and had a daughter, but we also know she loved young women deeply, as her poems reveal. They may have been her friends or students, worshipping Aphrodite together, and/or they may have been her lovers. Based on the evidence we now have, we will never know for sure. But from her birthplace on the island of Lesbos, and from the erotic content of her intimate writings, the term "lesbian" has arisen to describe the female form of homosexual love. A contrary tradition records that Sappho, heartbroken at being rejected by a male lover, leaped to her death from a high cliff beside the sea.

INVOCATION (2)

Come to me
here by thy temple,
where lofty apple boughs breathe in
the rising incense of altars,
where rushing rivulets sing through the branches,

and sleep, deep-shaded by roses,
melts through the leaves above
as meadow blossoms
bend in the breeze.
Come to me here, Goddess,
filling our festive cups
with tender grace.

In this invocation, the poet calls upon the goddess Aphrodite to attend the temple rites that honor her powers and the blessings she bestows. As a literary device, the invocation is as old as the channeler Homer, who invited the divine Muse to tell the sacred tales of Troy through the medium of his voice. "Sing, Goddess, of the wrath of Achilles," begins *The Iliad*, even as "Tell me, Muse," begins *The Odyssey*. No doubt before Homer, Greek priests had used such invocations to summon deities to religious ceremonies held in their name. Here Sappho summons a goddess to the shrine where her worshippers have gathered. The fact that Aphrodite was a goddess both of love and of the generative power of all life is signified by Sappho's evocative description of the shrine's sensual and natural setting.

A MANIFESTO OF LOVE (16)
Some say a host of horsemen, and others of marching men,
and still others of ships is the most beautiful thing
on the dark earth, but I say it is
whatever one loves.
It is certainly easy to prove,
for Helen,
the most beautiful woman in all the world,
left her brave husband
and went sailing off to Troy,

totally oblivious
of her parents and child
the moment Love led her astray—
so pliant are the hearts of young women
when stirred by Desire.
So am I reminded of Anactoria,
who is absent,
for I would rather see her strolling
with the sun shining on her face
than view all the gleaming chariots
and helmets of Asia.

In this poem Sappho reflects on the depth of her affection for a young woman named Anactoria. In contrast, the heroic world of Homer was centered on men and war. Here the poet issues a manifesto declaring a radically different set of priorities and sensibilities, one centered on women and peace. The cavalry, infantry, and navy with which the statement begins were objects of traditional masculine admiration, inherently destructive in their intent. As multitudinous entities, moreover, they stood and moved as impersonal groups. Sappho here rejects the traditional value system of the martial past by proposing a revolutionary personal calculus driven not by the desire for mass destruction but by the affection for a single individual. Helen of Troy is the thematic nexus, a woman caught up in a great war who gave, and lost, all for the sake of personal love. The glittering armament at the beginning of the poem is reflected in the shimmering, but tender, vision of Anactoria at the end. Yet rather than being a manifesto—a grandiose political term that Sappho herself might rightly reject—the poem is, in its purest sense, a simple expression of love.

Tongue-tied (31)

Like a god he seems to me,
that man who, sitting across from you,
listens attentively to your
sweet voice and
lovely laughter—a thing
that sets my heart aflutter,
for suddenly as I look at you, my voice
is stuck in my throat,
my tongue is tied, and a subtle
flame courses beneath my flesh,
my eyes not seeing, my ears
whirring,
sweat pouring down,
my whole body trembling,
my skin greener than grass,
and I just short of dying.
Yet all this must be borne since . . .

Seeing someone incredibly beautiful can leave the timid observer speechless. So it was twenty-six centuries ago. In this now-incomplete poem, Sappho describes what she experienced when, from a distance, she saw a young man sitting close to the young woman she loved.

In contrast, Homer never spoke in his own voice, describing his own personal feelings and needs. The later Greek poets did. For Homer, the subject was the epic past; for the lyric poets, the aching present. Homer might explore the emotions of an Achilles or an Odysseus; Sappho explored her own, detailing here the physiological symptoms of lovesickness with the observational accuracy of a hypochondriac. Note how the internal effects of love in this poem begin not with the eyes but with the very vehicle of poetry, the human voice. As Sappho hears her beloved's voice, her own becomes paralyzed.

BEYOND REACH (105)

As a sweet apple reddens on top of a tree,
on top of the topmost bough,
that pickers have missed
—no, not really missed, but could not reach . . .

Sometimes the object of one's love can seem utterly perfect, but because of that very fact unattainable. In this fragmentary half simile, Sappho compares her love to an apple. Greek epic made effective use of such similes drawn from the world of nonhuman nature to pictorially convey the characteristics of the human world. Thus a gathering of warriors is likened in *The Iliad* (2:87–93) to a swarm of bees. Here the first half of a Sapphic simile (the rest is lost) uses the image of an apple to suggest a sexually ripe young woman whom most prospective suitors have written off as unattainable. The apple itself was an erotic symbol associated with Aphrodite, the goddess of love, and appears elsewhere in Sappho's poetry (as in the first excerpt above).

NIGHT (169A)

Down has gone the moon
and stars, half-gone is
night, time passes
and I lie alone.

In this four-line stanza, perhaps a complete poem, the poet finds in the night an analogy to her own inner condition.

In ancient Greek, the word "kosmos" meant both order and beauty. What was orderly was beautiful; what was beautiful possessed order. Composed of but sixteen word units in

Greek—four for each line—this erotic stanza is a structural gem. The image of the moon having set (at the stanza's beginning) is reflected in the image of the poet lying down (at the stanza's end), while the half-gone night is set halfway through the stanza, bridging lines two and three.

The moon itself (feminine in Greek) was the realm of Artemis, a goddess always portrayed as virginal and chaste. The autumnal setting of the Pleiades (the "stars" of our translation) signaled to Greek farmers that it was time to seed their fertile fields. The poet is thus caught between sexual metaphors and their demands: she is a solitary virgin at a time she should be married and bearing children. Time passes, and she lies alone.

Regrettably, the astronomical information (a midnight when both the moon and Pleiades would have set) is not sufficient to permit us to assign a single and precise calendar date to the composition of this poem.

THEOGNIS

Born into an aristocratic family in the central Greek city-state of Megara, Theognis—like other members of his social class—suffered from the social upheaval that swept his country at the end of the Dark Ages, as a traditional economy based on landownership gave way to a new economy based on money. In the course of this economic revolution, people of "good breeding" were displaced in the social and political hierarchy by self-made men of business.

Of Theognis' elegiac poems (some 1,400 verses survive in couplet form), most celebrate the "old" virtues of honor and personal integrity and decry the supposed moral bankruptcy of the nouveaux riches. Some of Theognis' poems, however, are erotic in nature. While the first selection below is heterosexual in orientation, the majority of Theognis' erotic elegies treat the accepted aristocratic practice of pedastry, in which otherwise heterosexual males maintained physical relationships with adolescent boys.

PERSONA NON GRATA (VERSES 261–66)

Her parents no longer offer me wine
    now that her tender life is in *his* hands.
No, for *me* now it's just cold water, the kind
    she used to draw and carry—weeping over me—
from the well where once I took her by the waist, and kissed
    her neck as she arched it back, letting tender words drop from
        her lips.

This brief poem is extraordinary for its skillful deployment of contrasting images. The suitor the girl's parents favor is offered wine, but the poet is only given water. The favored suitor holds the girl's future in his hands, while the rejected suitor once held the girl herself in his arms. Last, water— a symbol of rejection in line three—becomes in line four a souvenir of lost romance.

BLESSED OBLIVION (VERSES 1335–36 AND VERSES 1375–76)
Blessed is the man who exercises in bed
    sleeping with a lovely boy the whole day through.

*   *   *

Blessed is the man who loves a boy, but knows not the sea
    and the way sudden night can overtake a mariner.

These paired poems and the two that follow reflect the Greek practice of pedastry, its perceived joys and its palpable pain.

HORSES AND BOYS (VERSES 1249–52 AND 1267–70)
You're just like a horse, boy. Now that you've had your fill of oats
    you're back again at my stable,
looking for your trusty old trainer, that meadow with the grass,
    that spring with the freshwater, those groves with their shade.

*   *   *

A boy and a horse think alike. A horse doesn't
    shed tears for its rider lying in the dust
but carries the next mount that comes along, as long as he gets
    his oats—just like you and your fickle affection.

ANACREON

(SIXTH CENTURY B.C.E.)

Anacreon is said to have been the first writer after Sappho to make love the main theme of his poetry. An inveterate lover of parties, he died at the age of eighty-five—according to tradition—after choking on a grape seed. Few of his poems survive intact.

ON EROS' ANVIL (48)

You whacked me like hot bronze with your ax
    and plunged me into an icy torrent.

In this fragment of a poem, Anacreon compares the Love-god to a metalworker cutting a heated sheet of bronze before tempering it in cold water. Anacreon is the metal, struck with the heat of passion, then suddenly chilled by emotional rejection.

THE POET STRIKES OUT (358)

"Catch!" yells golden-haired Eros
as he tosses a purple ball my way
(from the girl with the fancy sandals)
    and invites me out to play.
But—too bad!—the girl's from Lesbos
and the moment she sights my white hair
she makes eyes at another female
    and gives her catcher the air.

Anacreon decorates this brief trifle with an array of bright colors: the gold of Eros' hair and the white of the poet's own, the purple of the ball, and the colorful enameled tooling on

the sandals worn by the girl. In addition, he humorously in-
terweaves two erotic themes: the rejection of an old man by
a young girl, a commonplace of Greek poetry, and the less
common shunning of a heterosexual suitor by the lesbian
object of his desire.

THE ANACREONTEA

Modeled on the poems of the sixth century B.C.E. Greek lyric poet Anacreon, the sixty or so brief poems known collectively as *The Anacreontea* deal with wine, women, and song. They variously date, however, to much later times, having been composed—according to scholarly opinion—between the first century B.C.E. or C.E. and the fourth or fifth century C.E. As such, they represent a creative attempt to recast perennial sentiments in the style of an earlier age.

MY TIME'S NOT UP (7)
The women say:
" 'Anac,' you're old.
Pick up a mirror and behold
how your hair has flown away."
As to that hair,
whether it's here or there,
I can't declare.
But this I say:
"When Death is close,
why be morose?
Instead, let's kiss and play!"

Not every Greek poet was as depressed as Mimnermus (above) about the impact of old age on erotic gratification. For some, like the writer of this poem, impending death could even be an aphrodisiac.

A GREEK DON JUAN (14)
If you can reckon up
the leaves of every tree,
if you can tally up

the sands of every sea,
I appoint you
accountant-to-be
to tabulate my loves.
Take ten affairs from Athens
—no, throw in fifteen more—
then on to Corinth, where I've had
romances by the score,
because that's where the girls
are so easy to adore.
Farther east there's Lesbos and Ionia,
there's Caria and Rhodes:
two thousand extra-special
erotic episodes.
Keep up! There's much more to compile:
I didn't mention Syria yet
or my love boat on the Nile,
or Crete where they do it in theaters
and have orgies in the aisles.
I've had so many lovers
why ask what the total is?
I've had so many lovers
from India to Cadiz.

Love can be described qualitatively or quantitatively. This
poet chose the latter. Between the start and finish of his
erotic declaration, where he proudly implies his sexual ex-
ploits are innumerable, he leads us on a circular geographi-
cal tour of his world conquests (and of much of the Hellenistic
world), beginning in mainland Greece, proceeding east to
the Turkish coast, then south to Syria and Egypt, and finally
back north to the island of Crete. For the final measure of his
prowess, he spans the Hellenistic globe, from India in the
east to the Straits of Gibraltar in the west.

A MAIL-ORDER PORTRAIT OF MY LOVE (17)

Some six hundred portraits survive from the tombs and graves of Roman Egypt. Painted in a liquid wax that still retains its original vibrant colors, the portraits depict not native Egyptians but Greek and Roman immigrants who came to live in the thriving metropolis of Alexandria and its suburbs between the first and fourth centuries C.E. Their haunting eyes still stare out at us today from the walls of museums around the world, reminding us of their ancient humanity. In the following poem, a young woman orders an artist to create just such a portrait so as to capture the look of the young man she loves, but one who lives on the far-off island of Samos and cannot sit for his own portrait. A matching poem, in which a man orders a picture of his absent girlfriend, also survives (*Anacreontea*, 16).

I want you to paint my sweetheart Bathyllus.
Do it just the way I say.
Make his hair sleek
—dark underneath but
with sunlit highlights—
letting his loose curls
tumble down the way they do.
I want his eyebrows to be
darker than serpents
to underline his glistening brow.
Make his black eyes look fierce,
but temper them with serenity.
(The fierceness he gets from Ares;
the serenity, from the Goddess of Love.
At first glance you might be afraid of him,
but he's only thinking of what to say.)
Make his downy cheek

red as a rosy apple
—the blush of modesty perhaps.
I don't know how you'll do the lips,
so tender and persuasive,
but the mute wax will find the words
to make them speak.
After his face, give him a throat
more ivory than Adonis'.
Take his chest and arms from Hermes,
his thighs from Pollux divine,
his abdomen from god Dionysus.
And between those thighs,
pent up with passion,
paint a penis smooth
and growing with Desire.
It's a poor talent you have
if it can't also show his backside
to make the view even better.
And why should I have to tell you
how to do the feet.
Just name your price and I'll pay it.
In fact, toss Apollo's picture away
and hang Bathyllus' up in its place.
And if you ever travel to Samos,
ask Bathyllus to be your model
and repaint the Apollo you lost.

CLOSE TO YOU (22)
They say Tantalus' daughter
once became a standing stone,
and Pandion's child
took flight once as a bird.
Might I become your looking glass

so you could always gaze at me.
Might I become your dressing gown
so you would always be wrapped in me.
Might I become water
to bathe your body in.
Might I become perfume
to anoint your skin.
A pearl touching your neck,
a ribbon caressing your breast,
or even a lowly sandal
that by your foot is pressed.

> In this plaintive entreaty, the poet, craving physical intimacy,
> prays for some kind of metamorphosis that would allow him
> to be as near as possible to his beloved. In so doing, he
> draws erotic inspiration from mythic precedent.

No Goodbyes (32)

Let me drink a toast
—my head pillowed on lotus—
with Eros as my waiter
ready to fill my glass.
Life like a crushing cartwheel,
spins faster and faster,
and before we know it
we're a pile of bony dust.
Why waste libations on a tombstone?
Why spill out vintage on a grave?
Instead, anoint my body while I'm living
and splash roses on my flesh.
Eros, till Hades should call me
and bid me dance with the dead,
I'll scatter my worries like ashes
and warm my lover's bed.

A person needn't be dying or old to be acutely conscious of his mortality. That realization can make him, like our poet, want to drink life down to the last erotic drop while the cup is still in his hand.

A Wasted Education (52A)

Why instruct me in legalities
    and all of rhetoric's rules?
Why teach me grammatical niceties
    that are only good for fools?
Better to teach me to drink
    from the cup of Bacchus the mighty.
Better to teach me to play
    with golden Aphrodite.

Just as many a bored student has stared out of a classroom window on a warm and beckoning spring day, so the love poet reflects on the value of book learning when there are better things in life to do.

IBYCUS

(SIXTH CENTURY B.C.E.)

Tradition, idiosyncratic as it often is, records that Ibycus invented a three-cornered lyre and once fell off a chariot, breaking his wrist and making it hard to play a lyre, three-cornered or otherwise. We also learn that he was murdered by a band of robbers just as a flight of cranes flew overhead. Seeing the birds, Ibycus cried out that they would someday avenge his murder. Sure enough, some time later, his killers were attending an open-air theater when they saw cranes in the sky and fearfully reacted, attracting the attention of the crowd and provoking their interrogation, arrest, and ultimate execution.

SPRING (1)
Spring has come
and quinces and pomegranates drink
from the streams
where the nymphs' pure orchard is,
and vine flowers grow beneath tendrils
shaded in flourishing leaves.
But for me
love has no season of repose.
For flashing into fire,
Thrace's north wind of passion,
rushing with scorching
fury, dark, fearless,
grabs at the roots and shakes
my heart.

In this poem Ibycus contrasts the tranquil outer world of nature with the raging inner universe of human emotion.

Too Many Times Around the Track (2)

Once again Eros is giving me that look,
melting me with those hypnotic eyes
as he works his magic upon me,
luring me into passion's net.
As I see him coming, I tremble
like a champion racehorse past its prime
reluctantly approaching the gate.

> In this variation on the theme of love in old age, the poet de-
> scribes his unwillingness to enter the lists one more time.

EURIPIDES

(FIFTH CENTURY B.C.E.)

Together with Aeschylus and Sophocles, Euripides was one of the three greatest writers of tragedy during Athens' Golden Age. The plots of Euripides' plays were based on traditional mythic tales, but he portrayed his characters, especially female ones, with an unprecedented degree of emotional realism, making him the most modern of Greece's ancient masters of tragic drama.

THE PERILS OF PASSION (MEDEA, 629–33)

After securing the legendary Golden Fleece, Jason jilted Medea, the woman who had betrayed her family to help him achieve his objective. Now, to advance his career farther, Jason plans to wed another woman, whose father is wealthy and powerful. With compassion for Medea, a chorus of local women comments on the dangers of infatuation.

Love that is excessive bestows on human beings
neither goodness nor glory, but if Aphrodite comes
in moderation, there is no more welcome a god.
Revered lady, never let loose upon me the unerring arrow
of your golden bow, whose tip is anointed with passion.

In articulating the tragic implications of unbridled passion, Euripides' chorus echoes the famous Greek maxim "Nothing in excess." The ancient Greeks believed that going to extremes could be dangerous and therefore tried instead to practice moderation. But their intense emotional nature (so evident in the other extracts in this collection) made it impossible for them to avoid completely such self-induced suffering.

APOLLONIUS OF RHODES

~

(THIRD CENTURY B.C.E.)

Apollonius was a prominent citizen of Alexandria, Egypt, the cultural capital of the Mediterranean world during the Hellenistic Age. Indeed, for a time, he served as the head of its famed library. His greatest literary work was *The Argonautica*, an attempt to recapture the epic grandeur of Homeric epic by fusing it with Hellenistic sensibilities in a poetic retelling of the Argonauts' quest for the legendary Golden Fleece. To accomplish his mission, the Argonauts' leader, Jason, enlisted the aid of the sorceress Medea. (Their tragic affair had been depicted on the stage some two centuries earlier by the Athenian playwright Euripides [above].) In the following passage, Apollonius describes how Eros made Medea fall in love with Jason. His description of love's psychological and physiological effects bears the imprint of Sappho's introspective poem 31 (above), and would influence the Roman poet Vergil's later depiction of Aeneas' doomed lover, Dido (below).

MEDEA IS IGNITED BY PASSION (THE ARGONAUTICA, 3.286–98)

                           . . . Love's arrow burned
in the depth of the girl's heart like a flame. Again and again
she shot glances at Jason, while her anxiety
made her responsive heart beat rapidly in her chest.
Everything else faded from her mind as her spirit melted into
    sweet confusion.
Even as a woman spreads out twigs round a glowing firebrand
—a woman who labors at the spinning of wool—
so that under her roof while it is still night she may kindle
    a fire

soon after awakening, and the flame growing wondrously
from the little firebrand entirely consumes the twigs,
so, wrapping himself around her heart, Love the destroyer
blazed in her secret recesses. Her cheeks changed all over
from pale to blushing red, caught up in her mind's distraction.

MOSCHUS

(SECOND CENTURY B.C.E.)

ARMED AND DANGEROUS (I)

    In this poem, Aphrodite (otherwise known as Venus), posts a
reward for her missing son, Eros (or Cupid).

WANTED: CUPID, SON OF VENUS.
If anybody sees Cupid loitering around,
he's my slave, a runaway.
There's a reward for information leading to his arrest.
Payment will be a kiss from Venus or, if you bring him in yourself,
you'll get more than just a kiss.
The boy's well-known. You can pick him out of any lineup.
Complexion: not white but ruddy. Eyes: piercing and fiery hot.
Voice: sweet as honey. Doesn't say what he means.
Intentions: bitter as bile. A con man,
a complete liar, a sneaky kid. Plays rough.
Lots of curly hair and a look that's asking for trouble.
Hands like a baby, but they can throw things.
Can shoot an arrow to hell and back.
Naked body but hidden thoughts.
Winged. Flies like a bird from here to there.
Lands on men's and women's hearts.
Armed with a small bow and arrow.
Arrow's short but it can reach the sky.
On his back, a golden quiver. Inside,
those little arrows that have nicked even me.
All his weapons are dangerous, but the worst is the torch.
Not much light, but it can set the sun on fire.
If you catch him, tie him up, bring him here, and show no mercy.
If you spot him crying, watch out for tricks.

If he's laughing, drag him by the feet. And if he wants to give you
    a kiss,
look out! The kiss is bad news and the lips are poison.
If he says, "Here. Take my weapons,"
don't touch them whatever you do.
Those gifts are dipped in fire.

THE SEA (4)

The sea in the wind's caress
lifts my heart to leave the land,
to yield to her embrace.
But when her dark depths roar
—the foam curling above the rage of breakers—
I seek the shore and the haven of trees,
the kindness of earth, the branches
sheltering a lullaby beneath the wind's deep breathing.
Bitter is the fisherman's life, whose home is a ship,
whose toil is the sea, whose prey the wandering school.
Sweet instead beneath boughs to sleep,
to hear the close murmur of a brook,
blessing him who is still awake,
soothing.

> The poem describes the open sea as seductive but de-
> manding, capable of a sudden stormy violence that makes
> the tranquilizing waters of a gentle stream seem appealing
> by contrast. Though ostensibly about the external natural
> environment, the poem can also be understood as a de-
> scription of the poet's inner life: torn between two women of
> radically different temperaments, or perhaps torn between
> the turmoil of erotic passion itself and the peace of emo-
> tional solitude.

BION

(LATE SECOND CENTURY B.C.E.)

PRAYER TO THE EVENING STAR (9)
Evening star, golden light of lovely Venus,
beloved evening star, sacred jewel of the deep blue night,
as dimmer than the moon as you are brighter than any star,
I greet you as I go to serenade a shepherd.
Grant me your light to take the place of moonlight,
for the moon, newborn, has already set.
I do not intend to be a robber
or a highwayman in the night.
Instead, I go as a lover, and lovers
deserve all the help they can get.

THE ALEXANDRIAN EROTIC
FRAGMENT

(SECOND CENTURY B.C.E.)

Founded by Alexander the Great and honored with his name, the coastal Egyptian city of Alexandria rose to become the cultural capital of the eastern Mediterranean during the Hellenistic Age. Its Levantine population included a large percentage of Greeks who came to Egypt to live and prosper. The record of their everyday life has been reconstructed from papyrus documents unearthed by archaeologists from the city's outer suburbs. Among these documents is a piece of papyrus with the text of a contract in Greek drawn up in 173 B.C.E. The papyrus, however, was recycled, for on the back are the thoughts of a woman jilted by her lover. Though the original text is not composed in verse form, its rhythms suggest it may have been a poetic work in progress, an erotic "rough draft." Translated below is the first column of this "poem." Because of a break in the papyrus, the second column is too fragmentary to interpret. Yet what we have fully reveals the mercurial temperament of an idealistic young woman desperately struggling to cope with betrayal and rejection. If only love were as clear as a contract.

JILTED (COLUMN I)
The two of us had a choice,
and we chose to be together,
putting our faith in Aphrodite.
Whenever I remember
how he kissed me, intending all the while
to leave, causing confusion, I hurt.
Yet once affection became desire,
I could not banish him from my mind.

Dear Stars and divine Night, partner in my love,
convey me even now to him
whom Aphrodite made my master,
Aphrodite and the passion that seized my soul.
For a light to guide me
I have the fire blazing in my heart.
The fire's my torment. The fire's my pain.
That liar, who had the arrogance to deny
true love ever brought us together,
he is the one truly at fault.
And I, I'm going mad,
possessed by jealousy,
consumed by rejection.
Just throw me some flowers
to color my loneliness with.
My lord, don't send me away.
Take in one who is now shut out,
for I will gladly be your abject slave,
so desperate am I to see you.
(The hard thing is to be strong and tough.
They say if you give your heart to one man,
you'll lose your mind in the end,
for a love that is so narrow
can only end in madness.)
I'm not one to quit when
trouble comes my way,
but it drives me mad
to think I lie alone
when you're out
playing the field.
So let's call a truce
and make up.
Isn't that why we have friends,
to tell us who's been wrong?

THE GREEK ANTHOLOGY

The huge collection known as *The Greek Anthology* or *The Palatine Anthology (Anthologia Palatina)* consists of approximately nine thousand poems in Greek that date from the days of Sappho to the tenth century of the Byzantine era, embracing some 1,500 years of literary history. The name "Palatine" derived from the fact that a manuscript of the anthology was discovered in the library of the Counts Palatine in Heidelberg, Germany. The *Greek* or *Palatine Anthology* is actually an amalgam of earlier anthologies, the oldest of which was edited by Meleager of Gadara during the first century B.C.E. Apart from what their poems can tell us, many of the ancient "contributors" to the anthology are known to us by name only. Indeed, the authorship of many of the poems remains anonymous.

ADDAEUS
(DATE UNKNOWN)

THE DIRECT APPROACH IS BEST (10.20)
She's pretty? Then strike while the iron's hot.
    Just grab your balls and state your case.
But if you tell her, "I love you like a brother,"
    she'll slam the door right in your face.

ANTIPATER OF THESSALONICA
(LATE FIRST CENTURY B.C.E.–EARLY FIRST CENTURY C.E.)

LOVE ISN'T PRICELESS (5.30)
Everything that Homer said was true,
but this one thing above all:
that Aphrodite is golden.
For if you come with cash in your pocket,
no one, my friend, will bar the door.
But if you come with pockets that are empty,
a monster will block your way.
Thus does the rule of avarice
inflict injury on those in need.

PHILETAS OF SAMOS
(DATE UNKNOWN)

DEDICATION (6.210)

It was an ancient Greek custom to dedicate personal objects at a temple as an expression of appreciation to a god or goddess for favors bestowed, sometimes with the addition of a dedicatory inscription. Here the temple in question belonged to Aphrodite, and the worshipper was a recently retired courtesan or prostitute. The inspiration for this poem may have been pure invention, but another possibility is that Philetas was hired by a client (Nikias) to compose the verse.

At fifty years of age and more, sexy Nicky
    has hung up at Love's sanctuary
her pretty shoes and wig, and her polished mirror
    that shows exactly what it sees,
plus her expensive undies, and unmentionables,
    so you can inspect all the tools of her trade.

PHILODEMUS
(ABOUT 110–35 B.C.E.)

ON THE EDGE (5.25)
Whenever I lie on her bosom, whether in day
    or, more boldly, at night,
I know I tread on the edge of a chasm
    where I constantly risk my life.
Yet it never seems to matter, as long as Eros has my arm
    and pulls me ever onward beyond all thought of harm.

> Even when we clearly see the danger inherent in what we
> do, passion can override reason. In this poem, the night is
> viewed as more dangerous than day, perhaps because the
> woman's husband would be expected to return home and
> could catch the two lovers in bed. Of course, the poet notes,
> the woman herself, like the Sirens of *The Odyssey*, is a
> source of perpetual danger.

ULTIMATUM (5.120)
In the middle of the night, I stole away from my husband
    and came here, soaked to the skin from the rain.
Are we just going to sit here and make small talk
    or go to bed as Love's laws ordain?

> Philodemus here assumes the dramatic persona of a woman
> who demands her due from a lover.

ERECTILE DYSFUNCTION (11.30)
I used to come five or ten times in one night,
    but then I couldn't get it up once, try as I might.
Little by little this damned thing is dying

(not that it wasn't already half-dead),
and the way things now seem to be going
 I'll pretty soon be losing my head.
Considering the current state of my sexual woes,
 imagine what Old Age'll do when he finally shows!

RUFINUS
(ROMAN OR BYZANTINE PERIOD)

TOO LATE (5.21)
Didn't I tell you, "We're getting older"? Didn't I warn,
    "Love's assassins will loom"?
Well, they're here now: wrinkles, gray hair, dried-out flesh,
    the face drained of its bloom.
Does anyone drop by to see you at all,
    to flatter you in your room?
Or do they just give you a passing look
    as though you were a tomb?

    Aging, often regarded by erotic poets as a curse, has here
    become grounds for recrimination in the face of erotic op-
    portunities squandered.

BEAUTY CONTEST (5.35)
I just finished judging three asses. The girls didn't mind.
    They voluntarily showed me their heavenly behinds.
The first one was stamped with dimples
    that her plump buttocks were quick to disclose.
The snowy flesh of the second
    at its cleavage was pink as a rose.
The third was a wave on the ocean,
    undulating in gentle repose.
If Paris, judge of triple goddesses, had only gazed at mine,
    he would have declared them instantly incredibly more divine.

    The writer, focusing on a single trait of feminine beauty,
    likens himself to Paris, the legendary prince of Troy, who was
    once asked to choose which divine contestant—Hera (the
    queen of the gods), Athena (the goddess of wisdom), or sen-
    suous Aphrodite—was the most beautiful goddess of all.

SCYNTHIUS
(DATE UNKNOWN)

A PENILE REPRIMAND (12.232)

Now you stand erect, not languishing in anonymity
  but potent and confidently taut.
Yet you hung your head down in shame when he lay
  his whole body beside me, offering me all that I sought.
So rise up now, throb with emotion, and even drop a tear.
  A helping hand, I assure you, will certainly not be near.

In this anatomically graphic poem, the poet chastises his now
penitent penis for failing to perform when his male lover was
beside him in bed. In punishment, the poet denies his organ
the gratification it now craves.

STRATO
(EARLY SECOND CENTURY C.E.)

RIPENESS (12.197)
"Know the right time," said one of the Seven Sages,
    for everything is most desirable in its prime.
Even a cucumber in a garden is admired when first sighted,
    but, once ripened, is food for swine.

> The etiquette of Greek pedastry prescribed that a young boy
> be let go when he entered puberty. Here, the cucumber
> serves as a phallic symbol signaling such sexual overripeness.

AN EROTIC RIDDLE (12.210)
If two people are fucking
and two are being fucked,
how can only three be in bed?
(The one in the middle is screwing from the front
and at the same time being screwed from behind.)

Anonymous

Seasonal Fruit (5.304)

When you were an unripe grape,
you didn't even look my way.
When you became a ripe bunch,
you told me, "Go away!"
Don't begrudge me now
a taste of your shriveled
raisin.

The Greater Fire (12.17)

My heart is not warmed by women. Instead, it is men
    who ignite me and heap me with glowing coal.
Male fire is the greater, for as much as man is stronger
    than woman, so is my hunger for them more bold.

Love for Sale (5.2)

Sthenelais, the high-priced hooker, the five-alarm fire,
    who's always screaming, "Gold!" whenever she's for hire,
lay naked next to me in bed all night long
    gratifying me gratis till the break of dawn.
No more do I have to beg the bitch or so forlornly weep
    now that dreaming gives her to me so awfully cheap.

Metamorphosis on the Beach (5.83)

Would that I could be the wind, and that you, walking along
    the beach, could bare your breasts and press me against you as
        I blow.

A Lover's Prayer (5.11)

If Cypris, you save men floundering at sea,
then save me also from drowning,
shipwrecked as I am on land.

According to legend, Aphrodite, the goddess of love, was born at sea. When she emerged, she stepped ashore on the island of Cyprus, and henceforth was called Cypris, "the Cyprian." Because of her maritime birth, in addition to being the goddess of lovers, she also became the patron saint of mariners. Here the anonymous poet prays to her in that guise, shipwrecked as he is on the reef of a failed romance.

Erotic Love Poems

of

Rome

CATULLUS

(84?–54? B.C.E.)

Born in Verona, Catullus came to Rome during the last heady decades of the Republic, when the nation's democratic institutions were being tested by ambitious men who craved absolute power. He soon found himself in an elite social circle of patricians, where he fell hopelessly in love with another man's wife, very probably the willful and seductive Clodia, wife of Quintus Caecilius Metellus Celer, called "Lesbia" in Catullus' poems to veil her true identity. The best of Catullus' poems are about that affair, and it was an affair that—for tender-hearted Catullus—ended very badly. Yet through the vehicle of his poetry, Lesbia achieved literary immortality. Indeed, without *her*, Catullus never would have gained it for himself, for the Lesbia cycle has an intensity unmatched elsewhere in his writing. Regrettably, tradition does not preserve his poems in the chronological order of their composition, so reconstructing his emotional biography from them is hypothetical.

IN YOUR PRESENCE (51)

That man seems equal to a god to me,
greater than a god (if it be not blasphemy),
who, sitting opposite you, continually
    looks and listens

as you sweetly laugh, a thing that in my anguish
steals all my senses away, for as soon as
I look at you, Lesbia, nothing remains
    of my voice.

Instead, my tongue grows numb, and beneath my limbs
a subtle flame spreads, and a peculiar noise dins

in my ears as my eyes are dimmed
    in twin night.

Idleness, Catullus, will consume you,
an idleness you feed on and feast on too,
the idleness that has been the former ruin
    of wealthy nations and kings.

In this Latin poem Catullus imitates a Greek love poem that
was written six centuries earlier by Sappho of Lesbos, the
personal inspiration for the fictional name Lesbia that Catul-
lus gave his beloved. Whereas Sappho's poem 31 articulated
an attraction for another female, her verses are here adapted
to the purposes of Catullus' own heterosexual desire. Like its
literary model, Catullus' poem catalogues—up to a point—
the same physiological symptoms that Sappho delineated (a
loss of speech and sight, a ringing in the ears, and a flushed
feeling beneath the skin). Yet Catullus' departures are signifi-
cant: he does not speak of his heart fluttering, of his sweating
or trembling, or of his complexion growing pale—perhaps
because to a Roman poet such symptoms would have
seemed weak and effeminate. Catullus also exceeds Sap-
pho's original comparison of the man she envies by suggest-
ing that he may even be greater than a god, but then—in his
persona as a religiously scrupulous Roman—wonders if to do
so is blasphemy. In the final stanza, Catullus makes reference
not to his own imminent death (as did Sappho) but to the ruin
of great nations and kings—perhaps as a way of creating an
aura of grandeur around his own personal travail and simulta-
neously appealing to his Roman listener's sense of history. The
radical departure of Catullus' final stanza from its Sapphic
model, however, has in the past led some scholars to question
whether it really belongs to the rest of the poem we have or
comes from another by Catullus that is otherwise lost.

LITTLE BIRD (2)

Tiny thrush, precious pet of my beloved,
whether nestled between her breasts
or at her fingertip pecking
when it pleases her to play
her sorrow to allay,
tiny comforter of her hurt,
if only you could be my playmate too
and lift the care from my heart.

> The poet longs to be close to the beloved he has so far
> known only from a distance, and identifies with her pet, a
> male bird, which knows the physical intimacy he himself
> craves. Though in most English translations the Latin word
> "passer" is translated "sparrow," a sparrow would not by dis-
> position have been as likely a pet as a thrush.

PAVANE FOR A DEAD CANARY (3)

Lament, tender chorus of Cupids
and choir of tenderhearted men,
for my beloved's thrush has perished,
the precious pet of my beloved's heart
who was more dear to her than her very eyes.
Sweet as honey was he, and he knew her as well
as my sweetheart knew her very own mother,
nor did he ever stray from her lap,
but, hopping here and hopping there,
chirped to his mistress alone.
Yet now he goes down that shadowy path
from which no one may ever return.
Curses upon you, shadows of Hell,
that swallow all things that are lovely,
as lovely to me as was that thrush that you stole completely
    away.

Look, little bird, at what you've done to my darling,
whose weeping makes her eyes so swollen and red.

> In this plaintive dirge to a mock funeral, Catullus laments the
> demise of the pet bird he tenderly described in the poem
> above. Here Catullus points up its attentiveness and the ex-
> clusivity of the affection it gave to its mistress, qualities the
> poet himself would hope to embody should he replace
> the thrush as Lesbia's new vocally expressive "pet." Ancient
> sources tell us Lesbia's eyes were her most beautiful feature,
> and Catullus mentions them here twice.

HER PROMISE (109)

Sweet is what, my life, you called our love
    and swore it would last forever.
O heavenly gods, grant this promise be true,
    that her words come straight from her heart,
so we may spend our entire lives in loving,
    perpetually joined by a sacred bond.

> In what was surely one of his early poems, we see the hope-
> less purity of the idealistic young poet's love, a purity matched
> only by the simplicity of his language. Dominant in the
> rhythm of these verses are multiple spondees (metrical units
> of two long beats), which lend an air of solemnity not unlike
> the measured tones of a religious ceremony. Indeed, through
> this poem, Catullus was writing his and his beloved's (secu-
> lar) vows of affection.

DEFIANCE (5)

Let us live, my Lesbia, and love,
and not give a single damn
for the clucking of prudish old men.

Suns can rise and suns can set,
but once our brief light has faded
there will only be perpetual night.
Give me a thousand kisses, then a hundred,
then another thousand, then another hundred,
then another thousand, and another hundred more.
And when we've kissed our thousands, we'll erase the score
so we ourselves won't know,
nor someone else cast an evil spell
that is based on the count of our kisses.

In this fiery stage of his love affair, the poet simultaneously
recognizes and dismisses the fact that his adulterous rela-
tionship with his lover defies social convention. His solution
to the quandary of mortality is both passionate and mathe-
matically rational: to challenge the fact that he and his lover
have only one life by obliterating numeracy itself in an infini-
tude of kisses. Knowing the exact number of kisses—that is,
facing up to reality—might inevitably lead to the end of their
relationship.

ENOUGH (6)

Why wonder how many of your kisses, Lesbia,
would be enough for me and more?
Better ask how many grains of sand
lie in Lybia's drug-rich desert
between the hot mouth of oracular Jove
and the tomb of stammering Battus.
Or how many stars in the tight-lipped sky
look down on the secret loves of mortals.
So many kisses to kiss
would satisfy ravenous Catullus,
as many as prying eyes could not count
nor the evil bewitch with their tongues.

Like a pebble dropped in a pool, the idea of the kiss generates ripples of "mouth" images that run through the poem: the orally administered sedative silphium, which was harvested from plants that grew in the Libyan desert; the utterances of the oracle at Siwa; the tomb of stuttering Battus, whose very name (here "Batti" in the genitive case) resonates with the Latin words for kisses ("basia" and "basiationes"); the discreet, "tight-lipped" sky; sexually hungry Catullus himself; and finally the tongues of the jealous. Indeed, the very last word of the poem in Latin is "tongue," ("lingua").

I DON'T CARE (83)

Lesbia made fun of me in front of husband Jack
　　and gave the old fool a big laugh.
Hey, if she didn't mock me, Jackass,
　　it would mean that she didn't care.
All that noise just proves she remembers
　　and that ardor fuels her ire.

If the fictional Lesbia was really (as scholars believe) Clodia, the wife of Quintus Caecilius Metellus Celer, the composition of the poem dates to before the year 59 B.C.E., when he died. The Latin word for a dumb mule, "mulus," may have been a pun by the poet on *Metellus*' name, replicated in our translation by *Jack*ass.

TRAPPED (85)

I hate and I love. "Why do it?" you ask.
All I know is
I'm powerless to stop the pain.

Symptomatic of the poet's passionate condition is the simultaneous existence of opposing internal forces over which he has no control. The writing of poetry offers to him at least the temporary illusion of such control. By playing the clinician and engaging in psychoanalytical dialogue with an imaginary interlocutor, he is able for a time to distance himself from his own inner turmoil.

AFFIDAVIT (87)

No woman has ever been loved so much,
    I swear, as Lesbia was loved by me.
No contract has ever been honored so well
    as the pledge I gave you with my heart.

The ancient Romans were among the greatest lawgivers of ancient times. Here Catullus the Roman speaks as the injured party in a breach of contract suit. In the first two lines he testifies and addresses the imaginary jury. In the next two lines he turns from the jury to address—with a broken heart—the defendant, Lesbia herself.

RETURN (107)

If something he longs for and desires should ever come to a man
    who has lost all hope, nothing would ever be more cherished.
So cherished by me are you, who have at last returned,
    bringing something back to me more precious than gold,
returning to a man who has longed for you but long since lost hope,
    coming home to make his day a celebration.
What man could be happier than I, or name things
    more to be wished for in life than this?

REVELATION (72)

You used to tell me, Lesbia, Catullus was the only man who knew you,
    that you wouldn't even let Jupiter hold you in his arms.
I loved you in those days not the way an ordinary man loves a sweetheart
    but the way a dear father loves his very own sons.

But now I know you for what you are, and—even so—the flame
>   burns hotter
>   the falser and cheaper I know you to be.
How can this happen? Because such a wound drives a lover
>   to love even deeper the very thing he hates.

Even betrayal does not permit the poet to escape the war of
contradictory emotions he experienced early on in his love
affair (see poem 85 above). As in that earlier poem, a concise
psychological self-assessment generates a single key ques-
tion that the poet then seeks to answer. Yet the answer is not
curative but only descriptive of a chronic condition that must
persist. Few of Catullus' poems are more poignant or painful
to read.

EMASCULATION (63)

Though most of Catullus' poems are relatively short, at ninety-
three lines this one (here abridged) is among his longest. It
concerns the worship of Cybele, a nature-goddess of Phry-
gia in ancient Turkey, whose eastern cult had spread to
Rome in Catullus' time. According to legend, the goddess
had fallen in love with a young man named Attis (or Atys),
whom she wanted to retain to tend her temple. Though At-
tis swore to be faithful to Cybele, he later became enamored
of a nymph. In revenge, Cybele punished the two lovers by
cruelly killing the girl and compelling Attis to castrate him-
self. Thereafter, the goddess' priests were castrati called
"Galli," after the name of a local river, the Gallus, whose
waters—tradition said—had the power to make men mad.
Cybele's springtime festival, in which the myth was reen-
acted, involved orgiastic rites accompanied by wild, pulsat-
ing music played and sung by the goddess' ecstatic priests.
Catullus had spent a year or two in Bithynia, a land that bor-
dered Cybele's homeland, and had very likely seen the festival

in Rome. As a poet, he retold the tale of Attis, employing the hypnotic rhythm of the Gallis' song. But we may interpret the poem also as a personal tale: for Attis is none other than Catullus himself, psychologically emasculated by his cruel mistress, Lesbia. It is for this personal reason that Catullus has altered the tale, deleting mention of a mythic nymph and Attis' duplicity. Catullus' Attis comes to his senses over his infatuation with the goddess, but it is too late: the sexual damage is done as a result of his dedication and he is her prisoner for life, no good for any other woman. We begin where Catullus began, with Attis' arrival in Phrygia. Note the linguistic change in gender after the fateful act.

Borne across the sea's deep waters,
Attis sailed his speedy ship,
sped his steps through Phrygia's forest,
stepped into the shaded wood,
driven on by raging madness,
led on by an aimless mind,
took a sharp and stony sickle,
sliced the testes from his groin,
staining earth with dripping blood drops,
felt the penis now unmanned,
clasped a drum in snow-white fingers,
beat the hide with tender hands,
raised *her* voice in cultic frenzy,
sang aloud to *her* gathered band.

   [*In song, Attis urges his/her followers to worship Cybele, and then falls asleep.*]

When sleep assuaged the raging madness,
Attis dwelt upon her deeds,
comprehended all her losses,

sought her way back to the shore,
scanned the sea in tearful sorrow,
ached to see her native land.

[*Attis now regrets having castrated herself and longs to return home.
Learning of this backsliding, Cybele takes her revenge. As our excerpt
opens, Attis is finishing her lament.*]

When her lips poured out the message,
and heaven's ears drank up the news,
Lady Cybele let loose the lions,
ordered one to lead the way.
"Go," she cried, "and be ferocious.
Drive him back with fury's spur,
him who chose to shun my power.
Whip your tail across your back,
quake the forest with your roaring,
shake the mane upon your neck!"
Saying this, she loosed the harness,
let the beast release its rage.
Trampling brush, with paws it hastened,
reached the coastline white with surf,
found young Attis at the seashore,
fiercely charged and made her flee,
frightening her into the darkness,
there to be a slave for life.

[*Catullus concludes the tale with a prayer.*]

Divine Cybele, dreadful goddess,
keep your fury from my soul.
Drive others into madness;
let others lose control.

SPECIAL DELIVERY (II)

Furius and Aurelius, comrades of Catullus,
whether he ventures to India's far reaches
where dawn-lit beaches are continually beaten
    by the waves of a booming sea,

or goes to Hyrcania or effete Arabia
or to Scythia or Parthia the wild,
or to Egypt whose shore is always stained
    by the waters of the seven-mouthed Nile,

or whether he ascends the snowcapped Alps
to view the triumphs of Caesar's annals,
or traverses the Rhine and the choppy line
    of the barbaric British Channel,

you who are ready to face every challenge,
whatever the gods have in store,
take this brief message to my sweetheart of record
    and tell her the final score.

Let her live and be well in her obscene bed,
clutching hundreds of lechers to her loins,
loving none sincerely but orgasmically reeling
    while breaking the balls in their groins.

Let her not think of our love as before,
which fell by the wayside despite her vow,
like a flower that grew at the edge of a field
    that was touched by a passing plow.

The poem begins with a long mock-heroic (and sarcastic)
opening in which Catullus asks two acquaintances (whom he

elsewhere shows he has contempt for) to deliver a goodbye letter to the mistress he hates. The geographical sweep of the poem's beginning puts Lesbia in her place by diminishing her significance to that of a trifle. It simultaneously magnifies the poet's own hurt, zooming in from a whirlwind tour of the globe to a single fallen flower. The flower, of course, is Catullus himself cut down in his innocence by the sharp blade of Lesbia's insensitivity. Catullus is roadkill; Lesbia, the truck.

REDEMPTION (76)

If in any way a man can derive pleasure from the recollection of past good deeds
    wherein he deems himself to have done his duty,
and has neither violated a sacred oath, nor in any covenant
    taken the name of the gods in vain to deceive his fellow man,
many joys await you, Catullus, in the course of your long life
    from this unrequited love you had.
For whatever good men may speak or do
    these things have been said and done by you,
things that have, alas, been wasted on a thankless heart.
    Why then do you torture yourself more?
Why don't you seek deliverance by steeling your mind
    and obeying gods who do not want your tears.
It is hard to suddenly set aside a love of long duration.
    It is hard, but must be done in whatever way one can.
This is your sole salvation. This is the goal to achieve.
    This is the thing to do, however impossible it may seem.
O gods, if it is in your power to take pity, or if ever
    to some at death you grant redemption,
look down on me here in my misery and, if I have led a life that
       was pure,
    rescue me from this plague and this pestilence,
this torpor that seeps through my marrow
    and sucks all the happiness from my soul.

I do not pray for that other thing, that she love me in return,
  or what is less possible still, that she should be faithful.
I only ask that my body be healed and freed of this awful disease.
  Restore me to health, O gods, in return for the piety I have shown.

Oblivious to the legal status of adultery, the poet judges him-
self on a higher and, to him, more authentic moral plane: his
faithfulness in love. It is on that moral plane that he stands
and prays to the gods for the healing of his wounded soul.

VERGIL

(70–19 B.C.E.)

Vergil was thirty-nine years old when Octavian Caesar defeated Cleopatra and Marc Antony and went on to become Rome's first emperor, ending decades of civil war. In the political reconstruction that followed, Augustus sought a writer who could inspire the Roman people to dedicate themselves to building a new future through obedience and self-sacrifice. That man was Vergil, who transformed himself from pastoral poet to the author of Rome's national epic. Entitled *The Aeneid*, the epic is named for its central character, a hero named Aeneas who, after the fall of Troy, led a band of Trojan refugees across the Mediterranean in search of a new homeland. The land would be Italy, the future homeland of the Roman people, to whom the supreme god, Jupiter, had promised imperial glory. However, like Odysseus in *The Odyssey*, Aeneas had to face many trials and temptations before he could fulfill his mission.

Dido becomes obsessed with love

(The Aeneid, 4:54–89)

A storm at sea drove Aeneas' ships onto the North African coast, to a kingdom called Carthage ruled by a Semitic queen named Dido. Divine powers made Dido fall in love with Aeneas, but the human attraction between the two was seemingly inevitable. Both were strong leaders, both were widowed, and both had suffered and endured loneliness and the solitude of command. Like Calypso in *The Odyssey*, once she has welcomed the hero to her kingdom, Dido falls madly in love with the brave and handsome stranger who has landed on her shores.

With these words, passion inflamed her heart,
lending hope to a wavering mind and erasing all shame.
First, with her sister, she visited every shrine and prayed at the
    altars
for heaven's blessing. Then, following custom, they sacrificed sheep
to the gods of civilization—Ceres, Apollo, and Bacchus—
and above all to Juno, who guards wedlock's bonds.
Lovely Dido herself, holding the ritual cup in her right hand,
poured out a libation between a white cow's horns
and, as the gods looked down, frequented the altars
and consecrated the day with fresh victims,
poring over their exposed and palpitating entrails.
How blind seers are! How useless against obsession are
sacrifices and prayers! For a subtle flame consumes her marrow
even as a silent wound festers in her heart.
Driven to madness by pain, Dido raves and
roams mindlessly through the city, like a deer, unwary,
struck from afar by an arrow fired by a shepherd
who does not know he has hit his mark, and so she ranges
through the deep wood, the deadly shaft clinging to her side.
With Aeneas beside her, Dido crosses the walled expanse,
displaying the city's splendor and the projects under way,
her voice halting with emotion even as she speaks.
And as daylight slips away, she calls for another banquet
so she can once again hear his heroic tales
and hang enraptured on his every word.
Later, when they have parted, and the moon, obscured,
has veiled its light, and the sinking stars invite sleep,
she lies alone and sad in her empty house, the couch
where they sat empty, and, though he is absent
and apart from her, she hears his voice and sees his face,
or, captivated by the boy's resemblance to his father,
cradles Aeneas' son, counterfeiting the love she dare not speak.

The buildings no longer rise, the young men no longer march
or fortify the harbors and the walls against attack.
Half-finished, half-done, all work lies interrupted,
towers and cranes standing solitary against the sky.

> As the passage shows, love can be inimical to progress, for
> erotic obsession is self-centered, while civic progress de-
> mands rational concentration and personal self-denial. These
> are issues too that Aeneas will have to face if he is to live up
> to his historical responsibilities to his people and destiny it-
> self. In just the same way, Odysseus had to leave the self-
> absorbed and sensual world of Calypso's island if he was to
> fulfill his responsibilities to his family and countrymen.

DIDO AND AENEAS MAKE LOVE (THE AENEID, 4:160–72)

> On an outing together, Aeneas and Dido are caught in a
> storm engineered by the goddess Juno, who does not want
> Aeneas ever to leave Carthage and become the father of the
> Roman nation.

At the same time, a deep rumbling rolled across the sky,
and a rainstorm swept in with pounding hail.
The soldiers of Carthage and the young men of Troy, Venus'
    grandson
among them, scattered in every direction, fearfully seeking cover
as torrents of water hurtled down from the hills.
Together, Dido and the Trojan chief reached a cave's shelter.
It was then that Mother Earth and Maiden-of-honor Juno
gave their signal. Lightning flashed and the sky above bore witness
to their nuptials, and from the highest peaks the nymphs cried out.
It was the inaugural day for ruin and misfortune,
for Dido was moved neither by respectability nor convention
nor gave thought to the furtive nature of her love.
She called it marriage, and with that word she masked her sin.

The wildness and fury of nature signifies the essence of pas-
sion in the poet's eyes, for erotic passion is not subject to the
restraints of reason and can lead to destruction. The Roman
poet is also critical of behavior that ignores social conven-
tion and public opinion.

AENEAS ENCOUNTERS DIDO'S GHOST (THE AENEID, 6:450–77)

Prompted by a divine messenger, Aeneas realized his affair
with Dido had made him oblivious to his public responsibili-
ties and the divine mandate that he lead his people to the
promised land of Italy in order that Rome might eventually
be founded and grow. Unable to convince him to stay, Dido
committed suicide as he sailed away. Now they meet again
as Aeneas, still alive, tours the land of the dead and sees its
many ghosts.

Among them, bearing a fresh wound, Phoenician Dido
drifted through the deep wood. As she came near, the Trojan hero
recognized her dim figure amid the shadows, the same way that
at the beginning of the month, a man sees—or thinks he sees—
the moon overhead through the clouds.
Seeing her, he shed tears and addressed her with tender affection:
"Poor Dido, was the message I received then true
that you are dead and took your own life with a sword?
Was I then the cause of your death? I swear by the stars,
by the gods in heaven, and, if one may, by the dark depths of earth,
unwillingly, Queen, did I leave your shore, but by divine command,
those selfsame orders that now impel me to traverse the shadows
through desolate tracts and through deepest night.
Nor could I ever have imagined my departure
would have caused you such great pain.
Stop where you are! Do not retreat from my sight!
From whom are you running? These are the last things Fate will allow
    me to say."

With such words Aeneas tried to extinguish the fire blazing in her eyes,
but she turned her head away and stared at the ground,
her expression no more affected by his words than if
she were a piece of hard flint or a block of Parian marble.
Finally, she broke away and resentfully shrank back
into the shadowy forest where her former husband, Sychaeus,
consoled her in her sorrow and returned her love with his.

HORACE

(65–8 B.C.E.)

The son of a freed slave, Horace was given a gentleman's education by his dedicated father, who hoped that education would enable his talented son to rise through the ranks of Roman society. That hope was realized when Maecenas, the emperor Augustus' prime minister, became Horace's literary patron and close friend. Horace's poetry is marked by a consciousness of both his humble origins and his elite audience: in tone it is generally both urbane and gently self-deprecating, often expressing a love for the simple rural life that Horace had largely to leave behind in order to find fame in the big city. Most of his nonerotic poems are like versified conversations between civilized friends. Few of his poems are erotic in content, and fewer still glow with real ardor, but some blaze with sexual rage.

IN THE WOODS (ODES, I.23)

Why do you flee me like a fawn
that seeks in the trackless woods
its tremulous mother, frightened
    by the wind in the trees?

For whether a briar bush bristles
in the breeze, or a green lizard
bestirs a bramble, she trembles
    in heart and knee.

Yet unlike a tiger or African
lion, I do not mean to maul.
It's time, Chloe, to find a mate,
    not cling to your mother.

The imagery of this Latin poem by Horace resembles imagery employed five centuries earlier by the Greek poet Anacreon, who in fragment 51 compared a young girl to a frightened fawn (". . . meekly, like a young suckling fawn that, left behind by its antlered mother, was frightened"). Horace also addresses her by a Greek name, Chloe (meaning "young sprout"), to signify her tender youth.

REVENGE (ODES, 3.26)

The ancients often placed treasured keepsakes in shrines as symbolic gifts to their gods in thanks for past favors. Here Horace does so at the shrine of Venus, assuming the persona of an aging erotic warrior who has retired unwillingly from the battlefield of love. The object of his love is presumably the same Chloe addressed in the previous selection.

Not long ago I called myself a soldier
and campaigned with much success,
　　but to this wall I surrender my armor
　　　　and the lyre discharged from war.

To guard the sacred flank of Venus,
here, servants, lay out all my tools:
　　the axes, crowbars, and torches
　　　　that assaulted many a door.

O goddess, who reigns over sunny Cyprus
and Memphis barren of snow,
　　raise up your heavenly scourges.
　　　　Strike Chloe to even the score.

MISMATCH (ODES, 1.33)

You've got to stop bitching, old Tony,
about your two-timing girlfriend's baloney.

Stop singing sad songs in your beer
    about the young stud she now calls her dear.

That fox with the bangs named Eliza
has hots for Cy but Cy's eyes are
on Lucy, though even that lecher
    won't ever lay her, I betcha,

till a she-wolf starts fucking a bear.
Venus, you see, likes cruelly to pair
mismatched people beneath her yoke
    as Mother Nature's little joke!

I could have wed a socialite coquette,
but a maid swept me up in her sensuous net,
like a minnow caught up in the surging sea
    that rounds the curves of Calabria.

The original Latin of this modernized version is addressed
not to a "Tony" but to Albius Tibullus, a writer of erotic ele-
gies whom Horace knew and whose writings are excerpted
in this anthology. Beneath the poem's playful veneer is a se-
rious indictment of Love, charged here with using its powers
sadistically to attract us to the very people who are wrong for
us and can never truly meet our needs.

HOROSCOPE (ODES, I.II)
Don't ask what's wrong to know, my sweet,
what end the gods will will for you, for me.
Don't try astrology.
Better to take what comes:
many storms or—if God choose—that last
that now hurls down on crumbling cliffs
the winter sea.

Be wise: drink deep the wine.
Be blind to what the future hides,
for even as we speak life leaves.
Take today for all it is,
trusting little in tomorrow.

> The notion of savoring the moment, especially the erotic mo-
> ment, rather than planning ahead is encapsulated here in a
> Latin line that has become famously quotable: *Carpe diem*,
> translated here as "Take today for all it is," but literally mean-
> ing "Seize the day" (or even more literally, "*Pluck* the day," as
> though life were a flower in bloom that must be picked at
> once before it withers and dies).

HAG (ODES, 1.25)
How many pebbles
thrown by young lovers
strike your closed shutters
   now?

How many boyfriends
will pay for your favors
now that you're getting
   old?

How many suitors
will be serenading:
"I'm dying to sleep in your
   bed"?

Soon you will mutter
forlorn in the gutter
"I wish they all were
   dead,"

with the winter wind howling
and a demon moon scowling,
screeching of love and
    lust,

and your door will be flapping
as iced branches are cracking
and you shiver in that alley
    alone.

Beneath the veneer of gracious civility that covers Horace's
nonerotic poems is a deeper layer of sexual frustration and
anger that sometimes surfaces, as in this savage attack on
an aging courtesan. For another poem with a similar theme,
written in Greek in Roman or Byzantine times, see the works
of Rufinus above.

REPULSION (EPODE, 12)
What do you want from me, elephant woman?
Why do you send me presents and notes?
Since I've got a stomach that's weak,
seeing you is "puke at first sight."
Like a hound that can trail a pig,
I know a real stink when I smell it,
whether it's ooze from your nose
or "eau-de-goat" under your arms.
When a penis is flaccid and weak
and can't gratify her pent-up passion,
she works so hard to come
that a stench rises up from her flab,
and so much sweat drips down from her flesh
that it melts the makeup off her face
—white clay that was dredged from a pit
and rouge tinted in crocodile shit.

And she thrashes so hard with her lusting
that the canopy and bed are almost busting.
Yet with outrage she mocks my critique:
"Inachia doesn't exhaust you at all.
You can do *her* three times in a night,
but in *my* bed you fall flat on the job.
I hope Lesbia goes straight to hell
for selling me an impotent bull
when I could have had Amyntas of Cos
whose penis was harder in his crotch
than a tree trunk stuck in a hilltop.
Whom do you think I dyed
those sheets for in Tyrian purple?
For *you*—more than a wife would do
for a husband she calls her angel.
For my sake, why don't you just keep tryin',
and not flee like a lamb from a lion?"

TIBULLUS

❧

(55/48–19 B.C.E.)

A handsome aristocrat, Tibullus wrote two volumes of erotic poetry inspired by his love for two mistresses (called Delia and, ominously, Nemesis) and his attraction for a boy named Marathus.

A SIMPLE LIFE (1.1.43–48)

A small crop is enough for me, enough on a couch to recline,
    and on a bed familiar to ease my weary mind.
How good to hear harsh winds outside
    with a woman soft-held from all harm.
How good, when chilling hail collides,
    to find sleep in the warmth of her arms.

CURSED (1.5.37–44)

To heal my sorrow I've often used wine as a balm,
    but my pain converted every drop to a tear.
I've often locked another woman in my arms
    only to grow weak recalling you weren't near.
Then the other woman would call me cursed,
    and claim I didn't have a prayer.
A curse it was but not made of words, but of a face,
    tender arms, and blond hair.

MAGICAL CHARMS (1.2.41–58)

Whatever someone discloses, your husband won't believe.
    That's what a gypsy told me, consulting arcane leaves.
I've seen her hypnotize stars and charm them down from heaven,
    and raise corpses up from their moldy, abysmal haven.
I've seen her stop lightning bolts fast in their fiery tracks
    and lure pyre bones out from their ashen racks.

She can summon a spectral throng that's hellish in ilk
    or scatter them instantly with a sprinkle of milk.
She can dispel the gloomy clouds of winter from on high
    or make snowflakes flutter down from a summery sky.
She claims Medea's noxious recipes as her very own property
    and gave training in obedience to the savage dogs of Hecate.
She's composed custom-made incantations by which you can deceive:
    just chant them and spit three times if you really don't believe.
Thanks to them, your husband will discredit wherever he is led,
    even if with his very own eyes he sees us in your bed.
But don't sleep with other lovers or the results will be quite risible:
    after all, I'm the only one that can truly be invisible!

SULPICIA

(SECOND HALF OF FIRST CENTURY B.C.E.)

Sulpicia is the only woman whose poetry survives from the days of ancient Rome. She was the daughter and niece of powerful members of the Roman patrician class, and therefore highly educated. At least half of her eight amorous and coquettish elegies are addressed to a man to whom she gave the pseudonym Cerinthus. Traditionally, her poems have been appended to the collected poems of Tibullus, hence the peculiar numbering system used by scholars.

BIRTHDAY PLANS ("TIBULLUS," 3.14 OR 4.8)
My coming birthday: unavoidable.
A party in town: adorable.
On my uncle's estate without you: deplorable.
His insistence: unshakable.
My desire to be with you: insatiable.
So why must he be so implacable?

PLANS REVISED ("TIBULLUS," 3.15 OR 4.9)
My birthday party in the country is canceled!
That means I can be in Rome with *you*.
Now we can have a *real* celebration:
an intimate affair for two!

A CURT REPLY ("TIBULLUS," 3.16 OR 4.10)
With regard to your view that my love is precipitous,
let me thank you for being so terribly solicitous,
while chasing a career and a slut that's suspicious,
preferring her to the daughter of Servius Sulpicius.
There are many in Rome who are far more judicious
and call your sexual advances completely pernicious.

PROPERTIES

(54/47–2? B.C.E.)

After the death of his father and the loss of his father's farm, Propertius came to Rome as a young man in his late teens to find fame and fortune. Maecenas recognized his talent and became his literary patron; Vergil and Ovid became his literary friends. Propertius would gain immortality because of a woman he met and their tempestuous love affair that followed. In his poems the woman is called "Cynthia" to mask her real identity. Even after their breakup and, still later, even after her death, Cynthia continued to dwell in the poet's mind and caused him to write in order to exorcise her memory.

TILL DEATH DO US PART (1.19)

I am no longer afraid, Cynthia, of gloomy ghosts
    or the grim debt I may owe to the grave.
Having a funeral bereft of your love
    would frighten me more than those rites.
Cupid has not so faintly touched my heart
    that my dust would ever lose your imprint.
Though dead, Protesilaus remembered his wife,
    yes, even in the netherworld's depths,
and longed to fondle her flesh so much,
    he returned home a hollow ghost.
Whatever my spirit may be, it will always reflect your soul,
    for great love can cross fate's farthest reaches.
Should fair heroines there step forward in a chorus,
    those whom the Trojan War bequeathed to the Greeks,
none of them in my eyes would excel you in beauty,
    or—should a benevolent Earth permit
and destiny generously grant you long years—
    I would wet your aged bones then with my tears.

Yet as long as you live, please cherish my embers,
    for then death for me will have lost its sting.
What I fear, though, Cynthia, is an adverse love
    that may lure you away from my tomb,
and urge you unwilling to dry your tears,
    since a sweetheart, though loyal, can be coaxed.
Therefore, while we can, let us rejoice in each other by loving
    for there will never be enough time in life for love.

THE JOURNEY (3.21)

There is no turning back. I must go on to a land of reason
    to lose in distance passion's weight.
For it grows inside of me (even as I look at her), this hunger
    feeding itself and hungering more.
With all that I tried—hallways leading to
    nowhere—still the love-god's breath hangs upon my neck.
Scarcely—call it once—did she ever let me in (count all her no's)
    or came, and lay then sheeted in indifference at my side.
One hope remains: for, Cynthia, with this land behind me
    as far as you are from my eyes so far behind me will love be.
So come then, all hands push onto the sea my ship
    and each man take his turn at oars.
Wed glad sheet to outstretched mast
    for the breeze now assents to the prow.
To the skyline of Rome and to you, beloved friends, farewell,
    and to whatever you, Cynthia, are to me, farewell to that also.
So now I pay my respects to the rough-hewn Adriatic,
    fall on my knees before the pounding breakers' gods.
But after the Ionian will be crossed, when weary in Corinth's
    smooth waters my boat will have eased its sails,
the rest must you endure, my feet, to hasten the labor to its end
    where Isthmus shuts out with earth both seas.
Then, when the haven shores of Athens receive me,
    I shall mount the far reaches of Theseus' road.

There in Plato's pathways I shall find inner guidance
    or, Epicurus, in your delightful gardens.
Or I shall study Demosthenes' art, how the tongue can cut,
    or from Menander learn irony's smile.
And surely my eyes will find many paintings to feast on,
    or ivory-wrought—better, bronze-wrought—hands.
Thus the passage of years or the long, deep spaces of ocean
    will soothe the silent wounds in my heart,
or—if it be my fate—I shall die, not broken by base passion
    but in a sunset of honor.

> Like many a latter-day lover who has used travel as a way of es-
> caping and forgetting a failed romance, Propertius here sails
> to Greece to banish Cynthia from his mind. Yet even in his de-
> scription of the ship he sails on, erotic imagery looms as sail
> becomes bedsheet and raised mast a penis erect. Once in
> Greece, he plans to seek therapy in the rationality of philoso-
> phy (Platonic and Epicurean thought) and literature (the rheto-
> ric of Demosthenes, the gentle humor of Menander). In art he
> plans to find artificial surrogates for Cynthia's physical beauty.
> As he suggests, bronze statues of stalwart suntanned men will
> better heal his broken heart than ivory images of goddesses,
> which can only stir up memories of Cynthia's fair skin. The
> poem concludes with a prayer for psychological healing or,
> failing that, for an honorable death.

APPARITION (4.7.1–34, 49–54, 70–96)

> In a nighttime vision, the poet sees the ghost of his dead mis-
> tress.

Ghosts are real. It doesn't all end with the grave.
    A pallid shade escapes the snuffed-out pyre.

For Cynthia, it seemed, leaned over my pillow,
    fresh from her burial beyond the traffic's hum,
as I lay suspended between sleep and desolation,
    bemoaning the chill kingdom of my barren bed.
She had the same hairstyle she had worn that day,
    the same eyes I knew. But her gown was scorched,
and the beryl was melted on her favorite ring.
    Lethe's acids had etched her lips.
Her manner and voice were the same as when she breathed,
    but her brittle fingers creaked and cracked.
"Traitor (but what more should a girl expect!),
    does sleep already hold you in its grip?
Did you already forget all the subterfuges we used to use,
    and the window, worn by our nighttime maneuvers,
from which I so often hung by a twisted sheet
    as I came down onto your shoulders hand over hand?
We often made love on the sidewalk, our chests pressed tight,
    our cloaks laid out like coverlets to make the pavement warm.
Oh, that secret pledge of ours whose lying words
    were written on the wind!
Yet as my eyes were shutting, no one called out my name,
    or, at the sound of your voice, I would have gained another day.
No sentinel was posted to drive the evil spirits away,
    and the only cushion for my head was a roof tile of clay.
And, by the way, who saw you at the funeral bent over with grief,
    or marked you wearing a toga black and warmed by tears?
And even if it pained you to go through the gate, could you not
        have had them
    carry my corpse a little more slowly as it passed near?
Couldn't you in homage have prayed for breezes to fan the fire,
    or let my flames smell of costly incense?
Was it too much trouble to toss an inexpensive bouquet on top,
    or over the embers uncork a cheap jar of wine?

Yet I don't berate you, Propertius, however much you may
    deserve it,
    for on your pages, I admit, my reign has been long.
I therefore swear by the scroll of the Fates that none can unravel
    (and may Hades' three-headed dog not growl)
that to you I have been faithful. And, if I lie, may a viper
    hiss in my tomb and curl its coils atop my bones.
But now to some instructions, if you are of a mind,
    assuming another's magic doesn't hold you in its spell.
Make sure my maid Parthenia doesn't suffer in her declining years:
    she was good to you even when she didn't have to be.
My precious Patience, whose nature is reflected in her name,
    must never be made to hold another mistress' mirror.
And whatever verses you composed in my name,
    ignite them for me, and stop feeding off my fame.
Plant ivy around my tomb so its aggressive tendrils
    will bind together my crumbling bones, and at Tivoli,
where the apple-nourishing Anio irrigates the orchards' fields
    and ivory, thanks to Hercules' power, never loses its luster,
set up a column and on it inscribe, worthy of me, a poem,
    a short one, the sort a traveler may read as he hurries by from
        Rome:
'Here in Tivoli's soil lies Cynthia;
    her renown, Anio, has reached your banks.'
Do not, Propertius, dismiss dreams that come through hallowed gates;
    when such hallowed dreams come, they have import.
By Night we shades are wanderers; Night opens our prison's doors.
    Even snarling Cerberus roams about once the bolt is sprung.
The laws of Day demand that to Lethe's pools we must revert.
    We're carried back then, and the ferryman tallies his load.
Now other women may have you to hold, but soon you'll be all mine.
    Then bone will grind on bone, old lover, until we're finally one."
With that, as the recriminations ended,
    I reached out my arms, but her ghost slipped away.

The biblical Song of Songs declares that love is as strong as death, but the concept was never more chillingly expressed than in this poem. As in the previous selections from his work, Propertius is preoccupied with the idea of death, but here death is a dimension in which the unresolved erotic desires and conflicts of life are intermingled with guilt and forever perpetuated.

OVID

(43 B.C.E.–17 C.E.)

More verses of erotic poetry come down to us from the hand of Ovid than from any other poet of antiquity, Greek or Roman. Ovid lived in the affluent days of Rome's Golden Age, the age of Augustus Caesar. Ovid's "bestseller" then was a manual of seduction for men entitled *The Art of Love*. Originally written in two volumes, it became so popular that Ovid had to compose a third volume (just for women) to satisfy the demand of his female fans. The book's theme starkly contrasted with Augustus' avowed policy of reviving "family values" among the citizens of Rome. The resulting conflict combined with Ovid having inadvertently witnessed a sexual indiscretion in the imperial palace (perhaps by Augustus' own daughter) led to the poet's exile to the remote and barbaric shores of the Black Sea. Despite his plaintive pleas for pardon, he would never be allowed to return.

PYGMALION (METAMORPHOSES, 10.243–97)

The Metamorphoses had the most enduring influence upon the Western imagination of any of Ovid's works. It is a poetic compendium of mythic tales, mostly Greek, unified by the common theme of transformation. Many of the tales, like those of Orpheus and Eurydice, and of Pyramus and Thisbe, focus on love and its tragic consequences. One story that is an exception because of its happy ending is the tale of a lonely young man named Pygmalion, who eventually—despite his disillusionment with women—found his true love (or, more accurately, invented her "robotically" with the help of Venus). Many centuries later, Ovid's tale would inspire George Bernard Shaw to dramatically update the scenario in his comedy, *Pygmalion,* later adapted musically to the Broadway stage and Hollywood screen as *My Fair Lady.* As our tale begins, Pygmalion, offended by the promiscuousness of the women he has met so far, decides on a life of celibacy.

Having observed these women leading their lives in sin,
and shocked by the manifold vices of the female sex,
Pygmalion dedicated himself to a celibate existence,
and for a long time slept without a companion in bed.
During this time, he devoted his copious talents to sculpture,
carving from snow-white ivory a woman more beautiful
than any ever born, and promptly fell in love with his work.
It looked like a virtual virgin, a statue you'd think was alive
and one that, if modesty did not restrain, might even stir and move.
So is art concealed by art. As for Pygmalion himself,
he was consumed by a passion for this artificial body,
often touching his hands to it, as though to test his work,
wondering if what was once ivory might be ivory no more.
He kissed it and thought it kissed back, spoke to it, held it,
believing that its flesh yielded to his fingers when pressed,
fearing that such handling might even bruise its skin.
Sometimes he gave her compliments, sometimes brought her gifts,
the sort girls welcome: shells and polished stones,
little birds and flowers of a thousand colors,
lilies and painted balls, and tearlike drops of amber,
and even dressed her limbs in fine clothes,
placing rings on her fingers, a long necklace about her neck,
hanging pearls from her ears and trinkets from her chest.
It all suited her, but she in fact seemed the loveliest when naked.
So he laid her on a soft spread dyed in purple from Tyre
and, calling her his beloved, gently rested her head
on a feather pillow, as though she could feel on what she lay.
The day had come: the Cyprus-wide festival of Venus,

when heifers with curved horns overlaid in gold
bent their snow-white necks beneath the sacrificial ax,
and the smell of incense rose through the air. Standing at an altar,
Pygmalion timidly prayed: "If, beloved gods, you can grant all things,
please let me marry"—he dared not say "my ivory virgin"—
"let me marry someone *like* the ivory virgin I made."
Venus heard, since she herself was present at the festival
and knew what the prayer implied, and, as an omen of her favor,
made the altar's flame flare up three times as if to lick the sky.
Returning home, Pygmalion sought out the image of the girl
and, pressing his whole body against hers, felt her flesh grow warm.
Touching her lips with his mouth, fondling her breasts with his
      hands,
he sensed the ivory grow soft and surrender to his fingers,
just as, when warmed by the sun, wax worked under the thumb
becomes pliable from handling and takes on different shapes.
Though amazed, his joy mingled with the fear it was all an illusion.
Again and again he touched the object of his desire just to make sure.
It was alive! Her vein pulsed beneath his pressing thumb.
Then indeed did this hero pour out in fullest measure
his gratitude to heaven above. Finally, as he pressed his mouth to
      what was
no longer just an image, the ivory seemed to sense the kisses it now
      received.
Blushing, raising her eyes to the light, she now saw her lover against
      the sky.
The goddess attended their wedding, and when the crescents of the
      moon
had grown to fullness nine times, she gave birth to Paphos,
a baby girl from which the island gets its name.

MIDDAY (AMORES, 1.5)
      The sensuousness of Ovid's poetry is revealed in this selec-
tion from his collection known as the *Amores*, or *Loves*.

A heat wave and half the day already gone,
I threw my body on the middle of the bed,
the shutters half-open, half-closed,
making the sort of half-light you sometimes see in woods
when the twilight sun is sinking
or darkness is leaving and dawn is yet to come,
the kind of light shy girls might pick
to cloak their modesty in.
Then in stepped Corinna.
She wore a flowing shift,
her hair parted and loose about her neck,
the way men say Queen Semiramis used to look
or Lais, the courtesan so many loved.
I tore the shift right off.
No matter: it was transparent anyway.
But she fought to keep it on and,
since she battled like she wished to lose,
it wasn't hard to win.
She stood there before me naked,
and my scanning eyes could find no flaw:
the shoulders and the arms,
the curving breasts that asked to be pressed,
the smooth stomach beneath their fall,
the faultless hips and youthful thighs. . . .
But why itemize? I saw nothing I did not like
and squeezed her flesh into my own.
You can guess how it ended: both of us worn-out
and lying side by side.
If only other middays might grant me such a prize.

Ostensibly the description of an assignation on a summer af-
ternoon, the poem is also an elaborate exposition on duality.
First there is one (Ovid alone); then another (his mistress,
Corinna) appears. Such elemental human mathematics are

foreshadowed by the time and place at which the lovers meet: Ovid lies in the middle of a bed in the middle of a day, one shutter open, one closed, filling the room with half-light like the light that mediates between day and night. Even Corinna, when she enters, is described dualistically. Her delicate garment is neither properly on nor truly off; her hair sweeps down symmetrically to either side of her neck; and she is likened to twin exemplars of feminine beauty. With her garment removed, it is the middle of her body that Ovid then describes, the part—once covered—between her shoulders and her thighs. Within each of the lovers, there is a dual nature as well. Corinna's entrance follows immediately upon mention of virginal modesty, yet she is soon compared to a courtesan and her efforts to retain her garment are halfhearted. Ovid also occupies a middle ground: cataloguing in sensual detail the parts of Corinna's naked body, but stopping short of the genital area to which his catalogue leads. The poem ends as it began, only now two lie on the bed where one had lain before.

ABORTION (AMORES, 2.13[14])

While rashly discharging the cargo of her laden womb,
    Corinna lies weakened, barely clinging to life.
Without ever telling me, she risked such great danger
    and merits my anger were anger not trumped by fear.
(I either made her pregnant or assume I did:
    with me, often what can happen usually does.)
Isis, tender of the western delta and Canopus' fertile fields,
    guardian of Memphis and Pharos full of palms,
where the swift Nile glides down on its broad-based bed
    and slips through seven harbors into the waves of the sea,
I pray by thy sacred rattles and Anubis' awesome face
    (may Osiris pay loving attention always to thy rites,
and the slow serpent slide across thy sanctuary's floor,
    and in thy procession the horned Apis-bull parade),

look down and show forbearance not just on one but on two,
    for, in giving life to my mistress, thou wilt be giving life to
      me too.
Often she patiently attended the sacrifices on thy festival days
    at the shrine where Cybele's eunuch priests brush by thy laurel.
Do thou, who hast before shown pity to girls in labor
    whose hidden weight stretches their bodies that are slowed,
be kind and grant my prayer, goddess of childbirth, Ilithyia,
    for she is the sort worthy to serve thee someday.
I myself, wearing white, shall burn incense at thine altar;
    I myself shall lay votive offerings at thy feet,
adding: "Ovid gives thanks for Corinna's salvation."
    Just make room for the inscription and offerings I shall give.
Finally, if it is right to offer advice amidst my fear,
    make this the last time you take such risks, my dear.

Documentary evidence suggests that abortion may have
been a not uncommon practice for women in imperial Rome.
Here the poet prays for his mistress' recovery from such a
procedure. In so doing, he calls upon the Egyptian goddess
Isis, whose cult had traveled to Rome and who was regarded
as a guardian of women in childbirth. Egyptian Isis was iden-
tified with the power of life as was Egypt itself with the
power of fertility and natural productivity, themes that the
poet symbolically interweaves with the description of his
mistress' physiological condition. The poet also prays to
Ilithyia, a goddess of childbirth whose worship had origi-
nated in Greece.

BY LOVE COMMANDED (AMORES, 2.9B)

If God commanded, "Thou shalt live but not love,"
    I'd disobey, for girls are too sweet a sin.
When my passion is all spent and the ardor in my heart has subsided,
    the whirlwind in my tormented brain inexplicably drives me on.

Like a rider pulling back in vain on the foaming bit
    of a tough-mouthed horse galloping headlong,
like a ship about to drop anchor in a safe haven
    suddenly swept back onto the high seas by a squall,
I am carried back on Cupid's fickle breezes,
    stung again by Love's notorious darts.
Shoot me, boy! Before your bow I offer myself up naked.
    You hold the power. It's in your hands.
Those arrows don't even need to be aimed. They already know
      the way.
    In fact, they know me better than the quiver they call home.
I pity the man who manages to lie alone in bed
    night after night and calls sleep a blessing.
Fool! What is sleep but death's chill twin?
    Fate will grant us time enough for rest.
Sometimes I may be duped by my sweetheart's lies
    (but hoping they're true gives me pleasure).
Sometimes she may flatter me, sometimes pick a fight.
    There are times I enjoy her body, and times she throws me out.
If Mars is unpredictable, Cupid, he gets it from you,
    his stepson, and follows your example in wars.
Your behavior is capricious, more flighty than your wings.
    The joys you bestow are bittersweet; your promises, flavored with
      lies.
Nevertheless, if induced by your lovely mother, you show me favor,
    I shall grant you grudging dominion over my heart.
Add females to your domain, inconstant as is the breed,
    and you'll double the number of adherents to venerate your creed.

THE COLLEGE OF EROTIC KNOWLEDGE (THE ART OF LOVE, 1.1–66)

In Ovid's day, *The Art of Love (Ars Amatoria)* was both the
poet's most popular work and his most controversial. It is
also the world's first sexual self-help book, a handbook for
men on how to begin and sustain a love affair. That such a

book should have been written is a natural consequence of the audience Ovid addressed: an affluent and leisured upper class who delighted in sensual pleasure during an age that Ovid himself called "golden." In addition, the perpetually practical bent of Roman culture created a ready market for such a how-to book. Here are *The Art of Love*'s opening verses.

If anyone here isn't skilled in the ways of loving,
    let him read this poem and, after learning, love.
By skill are swift ships steered with oar and sail;
    by skill, fast chariots driven; over love too must skill prevail.
With horses and taut reins Automedon, Achilles' driver, was equipped,
    and captain Tiphys manned the helm of the Argonauts' ship.
When it came to mastering Cupid, Venus gave me the chance,
    so just call me the Tiphys and Automedon of romance.
Wild is he and may often prove resistant,
    but he's a boy, teachable with talent latent.
Chiron practiced young Achilles on the lyre,
    and tamed the youth's fiery passion and ire.
He who terrified enemies and friends untold
    trembled, they say, before a man quite old.
The hands Hector would someday feel, Achilles held out to be whipped,
    under that persistent centaur's tutorship.
As Chiron cured Achilles of rashness, I'll cure Cupid of brashness.
    Each was a savage boy; and each from a goddess born.
Notwithstanding, the plow wears down the neck of the bull,
    and the teeth of proud horses are ground by the bit.
So Cupid will yield to me, however much he may scorch
    my heart with flaming arrows and brandished torch.
The more Cupid abused me, the more he violently used me,
    the better an avenger of his wounds I shall be.
I shall not counterfeit the arts you taught me, Apollo,
    nor obey the feathery portents of a heavenly swallow,

nor claim to have had a visitation from Muses divine
  while herding sheep on mystic Ascra's grassy incline.
No, this work is based on reality; it's the teachings of experience you'll
    hear.
  The truth and only the truth is my subject, so be seated, mother
    Venus, and lend an ear.
As for the prudish, keep your proper distance and don't get overly
    near.
  No delicate chaplets or toe-touching robes are in vogue here.
I shall sing of sex that is harmless, of stealing that is absolutely
    allowed,
  and everything I sing of will be legal. It's not a crime, I vow.
First: whatever you aim to be loving, you must make an effort to
    secure,
  you who have just enlisted as a soldier in Ovid's erotic corps.
The next phase of your mission is seduction: to sleep with the girl
    you've pleased.
  Third, make sure you'll militarily hold whatever ground you've
    seized.
See the tracks left by my chariot? All you have to do is follow my lead.
  Just make sure, as you round the goalpost, by it your wheels will
    squeeze.
But if you have time with loose reins in your hands to cruise,
  carefully survey your options before it's time to choose.
Your "one and only" won't fall into your arms after tumbling through air.
  The girl who suits your discriminating taste must be caught with
    flair.
The good hunter knows where to set his snares for deer,
  knows into what glade the gnashing boar will veer.
The good fowler knows his bushes; the fisherman, detours,
  in what out-of-the-way waters to drop seductive lures.
You too must seek the subject for your amorous events,
  scout out the terrain, and learn the places she frequents.

I shall not order you to set sail while you're waiting for a wind,
    nor insist you travel before you're packed and ready to begin.
Even if Perseus carried off Andromeda from the swarthy Indians
    and that Hellenic girl Helen was abducted by a Phrygian,
there are so many pretty girls for the taking right here in Rome,
    you'll say, "This city's got everything!" and add, "Why ever roam?"
As many wheat fields as are in Troy, as many vineyards as are on Lesbos,
    as many fish as are in waves, as many birds as are in leaves,
as many stars as are in the heavens, so many girls does Rome possess.
    It's no accident Venus makes Rome her permanent address.
If you're charmed by girls still in their growing years,
    the selection offered will reduce your eyes to tears.
If you like your women young, there are thousands you can choose,
    in fact, a number so awesome it's likely to confuse.
Or if you prefer them mature and of a much wiser age,
    the list of names will run right off the written page.

WHERE THE GIRLS ARE (THE ART OF LOVE, 1:89–132)
A prime spot to do your hunting is the theaters' curving rows,
    settings where you'll find that your satisfaction grows.
You may find true love or an affair not very deep,
    something you might sample once, and something you may want
        to keep.
As ants march and return in one continuous line,
    clutching in their mouths the grain on which they dine,
or as bees in the air over meadows will climb
    after buzzing fragrant flowers and waving thyme,
sophisticated women progress to the crowded shows,
    so many my confusion is easy enough to know.
They come to see, and come in order to be seen.
    It's the downright ruination of innate decency.
You were the first, Romulus, to provide a dramatic escape
    by giving your men a famous Sabine rape.

Awnings didn't then hang from a marble theater
 or saffron bathe a stage in its bright color.
A shady Palatine with leaves that were numberless
 supplied the kind of scenery that lacked for any artifice.
The audience sat on seats that were made of sedge
 as foliage spread over their shaggy unkempt heads.
They scanned the crowd, each picking out the kind
 of girl he wanted, conspiring in his mind.
While the piper blew the rhythm on his flute
 and the dancer stomped the floor with his foot,
in the midst of the noise (they didn't have "applause"),
 the king gave the signal to incite their joint cause.
All at once, they gave a leap, revealing their ambition
 to accomplish with lusting hands their devirginizing mission.
As timid doves flee the eagles' flock,
 as tender lambs flee the wolves' dense pack,
so they panicked at the onslaught of the men,
 bleached of the color they had before then.
There was universal fear, but fear lacked one face.
 Some tore their hair; others stared into space.
One sat in silence; another cried, "Mamma!" in dread.
 One screamed; one sat dumb; one stayed; one fled.
The captive girls were led off, a luscious prize,
 and fear itself made them more attractive in many men's eyes.
If any fought back too much and resisted harm,
 her man picked her up in his eager arms,
and said: "Why spoil those lovely eyes with a tear?
 Your father, like I, once held a bride this near."
Romulus, you knew how to give your soldiers rewards.
 Give them to me too and I'll serve in your wars!

To appeal to his Roman audience, Ovid here draws upon an
existing legend that told how Romulus, Rome's founder, rec-
ognized that he and his followers would need women if they

were to propagate a new race. To solve the problem, tradition related, Romulus invited neighboring tribes to a founders' festival and used the occasion to kidnap the native women his mission required. In this revered myth, we see how the themes of sex and violence were interwoven in the Roman mind. The military mentality of Roman society is also evident in the image of the lover as soldier, campaigning for erotic conquest and sexual gratification. In this excerpt from *The Art of Love*, Ovid co-opts Romulus into his literary scheme by appointing him the patron saint of seduction, thereby establishing an historic and patriotic precedent for the erotic behavior he encouraged in the males of his own day.

MAKE THE MOST OF WHAT YOU'VE GOT
(THE ART OF LOVE, 3.769–812)

The success of the first two volumes of *The Art of Love*, which were aimed at a male audience, inspired Ovid to write a third volume, even more sexually explicit, for women. Here are its concluding verses.

Things that make one blush must now be added to the tally
    but, according to Venus, that's right up my alley.
Let "Know thyself" be your rule. Whether you're short or tall,
    let your body be the director, since one size won't fit all.
So if your face is pretty, give him a frontal close-up,
    but if your rear is prettier, then make it "bottoms up."
Milanion supported Atalanta's legs on his shoulders,
    for from that angle he preferred to behold her.
Only petites should ride on horseback. So, fearing he'd eject her,
    stout Andromache wouldn't mount upon her Hector.
A woman whose figure and flanks are still nubile
    should kneel on the bed and pose in profile.
If she has firm thighs and breasts without flaw,
    by lying sideways she'll make him stand in awe.

Loosen your long hair with a wild Thracian flair
    to spill out your tresses and leave your neck bare.
And if pregnancy has marked your belly with lines,
    flip over and point out your buttocks' design.
Want magic? Here's a simple trick that needs no knack:
    just lie on your side, a little bent back.
Neither the tripods of Phoebus or the horns of great Ammon
    will tell you more truth than this Muse-ified shaman.
So trust in my art, which derives from experience.
    It's not my intention to cause you inconvenience.
Let a woman who has come feel it deep in her marrow,
    for two not just one should caress Cupid's arrow.
May tender words and soft murmurs be loving's mainstay,
    nor wanton words be absent in the midst of foreplay.
And you to whom Nature has denied Venus unbound,
    imitate sweet joys with a counterfeit sound.
(Unfortunate is the girl who cannot employ
    that spot male and female together should enjoy.)
Only take care that your pretense is not obvious
    by feigning looks and moves that appear spontaneous.
Passionate breathing may obscure your designs,
    though your vagina may disclose its own secret signs.
She who demands a big gift after sex
    is just asking for him to make her his "ex."
And don't open the blinds when you lie on the bed;
    there are anatomical things that are better left unsaid.
Now that the race is run, I step down from the swans
    that have drawn the chariot I have ridden upon.
Let this graduating class in whom I take pride
    inscribe on their loving cup: "Ovid was our guide."

MARTIAL

(38/41–101/104 C.E.)

Martial came from his birthplace in Spain to seek his fortune in Rome. He prospered by using his literary talent to sing the praises of the emperors, flatter the rich, and satirically skewer their mutual enemies. His poetic specialty was the concise epigram, and he wrote well over a thousand, including some that celebrated the grand opening of the Colosseum. Few of his poems are explicitly sexual, but those that are cover crude sensibilities with a polished stylistic veneer.

POPULARITY (6.40)
You've always been my number one, Lycoris,
  but lately you've become number two.
What you *used to be* to me, Lycoris, Glycera currently *is*.
  You I once *wanted*, but her I now *want*: funny what time can do.

ORDERS (6.23)
You're always ordering me to get my penis up,
  but a dick isn't a finger that can point.
No matter what your hands and words may do,
  it's your face that gets me out of joint.

DISQUALIFIED (3.32.1-2)
Never take an old woman to bed?
  Truth be told, I sometimes do.
But that simply doesn't apply to you
  because you're not old—you're dead!

POMPEIIAN GRAFFITI

(BEFORE THE CITY'S DESTRUCTION IN 79 C.E.)

Later reclaimed from volcanic dust by modern archaeology, the Neapolitan town of Pompeii was buried by the eruption of Mount Vesuvius in 79 C.E., and became an instant time capsule of ancient Roman life. Among its remains were the writings on its walls, ranging from professionally executed advertising signs to casual notes scribbled by friends. Occasionally, a bit of poetry survived, including this anonymous four-line philosophical commentary on the ephemeral nature of love, written on a wall along the Via dell' Abbondanza ("Easy Street"). Fittingly, soon after the poem was discovered and copied, the plaster on which it had been written crumbled, erasing its words for all time.

IMPERMANENCE (CORPUS OF LATIN INSCRIPTIONS, 9123)
Nothing can last for all eternity.
Noonday suns shimmer and sink in the sea.
Moons waxing full in the sky must wane.
Passionate love will run off like rain.

THE PERVIGILIUM VENERIS

(EARLY FOURTH CENTURY C.E.?)

It is altogether fitting that the final selection in this anthology should celebrate the spring, for at the heart of romantic love is the essence of beginnings. The title in Latin means "The All-Night Vigil of Venus" and suggests, together with its content, that the poem was inspired by a nocturnal Roman festival celebrating the coming of spring and honoring the goddess through whose divine powers the world of nature was seasonally reborn. The central erotic metaphor of this excerpt is the rosebud, virginal until aroused by wetness and warmth, at which time it opens to reveal its previously hidden but vibrant interior. The date of the poem is uncertain (dates in the second and early fourth centuries have been argued) and the author is anonymous (though the name of a fourth century poet named Tiberianus has been proposed). What is certain is that the poem is no impersonal hymn, for in its closing verses the anonymous poet poignantly discloses the personal disconnect he feels between the generative promise of spring and his or her own loneliness. Such a sentiment had been voiced a thousand years earlier by the Greek poet Ibycus, and would be again more than a thousand years later, albeit more darkly, by T. S. Eliot, who would call April "the cruellest month."

ODE TO VENUS (1–27; 89–93)

Tomorrow let the loveless find her lover; let him who loved once, love again.
Spring is here, and spring is singing; spring is when the world is born.
Spring is longing and longed embracing; spring is mating time for birds.
Spring is leafy curls unfurling as wedding showers wet the woods.
She who couples lovers lying, shaded 'neath the boughs of trees,

weaves their greening, living bower from the myrtle's verdant shoots.
Tomorrow Venus issues orders, seated on her sublime throne.
Tomorrow let the loveless find her lover; let him who loved once, love again.
Once did sea from blood celestial in a foaming mass create
midst the azure crowds of creatures, midst the herds of two-hoofed
    steeds,
Venus rising up from billows, climbing on the crests of waves.
Tomorrow let the loveless find her lover; let him who loved once, love again.
She herself adorns the season, painting it bright with crimson gems,
stimulates the stems' warm nipples, blowing with the West Wind's
    breath,
till they grow to buds that burgeon. She herself takes liquid dew
left behind by night's departure, sprinkles moisture far and wide,
shaping tears that droop and dangle, hanging from their heavy weight,
droplets leaning from their roundness, holding back their final fall.
How the deep red flowers are blushing, revealing maidens' modest
    ways!
Moisture which the stars in heaven gather on eves that are serene
in the morning unpeels blossoms sheltered in their dampened sheaths.
She herself commanded virgin roses should at dawn be plucked.
Made of blood from divine Venus and kisses straight from Cupid's
    mouth,
wrought from rubies, flames of fire, and flaring rays of blazing suns,
on the morrow what was hidden in her maiden's fiery robe
she will feel no shame disclosing, wedded in a unique bond.
Alas, *she* sings, but *I* am silent. When will *my* spring finally come?
When shall I become the swallow, so my muteness I may end.
I have lost my Muse through silence; nor will Phoebus show regard.
So the people of Amyclae, being tongueless, through their quiet were
    undone.
Tomorrow let the loveless find her lover; let him who loved once, love
    again.

TRANSLATOR'S ENVOI

(AFTER STRATO, EARLY SECOND CENTURY C.E.)

Years hence some reader may perchance
assume these loves reflect my own.
Yet fantasy's seeds are often sown
by a publisher's generous advance.

GLOSSARY

ACHAEANS: Homeric name for the Greeks

ACHILLES: bravest Greek warrior to fight at Troy

ACTORIS: a maid who served Penelope

ADONIS: handsome young man loved by Aphrodite

AENEAS: Trojan prince, the son of Venus and Anchises

AEGIS: a shieldlike emblem carried or worn by Zeus and Athena to frighten away enemies

AJAX: name of two warriors who fought on the Greek side at Troy

ALCIPPE: Marcus Argentarius' sweetheart

ALEXANDER: Trojan prince beloved by Helen, also called Paris

AMMON: god of the Egyptian state whose oracle was located in the western desert

AMYCLAE: a city near Rome that, according to legend, had outlawed rumors and, when a real enemy approached, perished because of its enforced silence

AMYNTAS OF COS: a supposed rival of Horace

ANIO: a river that cascades down from Tivoli

ANUBIS: jackal-headed Egyptian god of funerals and cemeteries

APIS-BULL: bull sacred to Egyptian religion

AURELIUS: an acquaintance of Catullus

AUTOMEDON: Achilles' charioteer during the Trojan War

ANACTORIA: young woman beloved by Sappho

ANCHISES: a member of Trojan royalty and the father of Aeneas

ANDROMACHE: wife of the Trojan warrior Hector

APHRODITE: Greek goddess of sexual attraction and love, known to the Romans as Venus

APOLLO: Greek god of prophecy and patron of the arts

ARES: Greek god of war

ARGOS: a district in the southern part of Greece

ARGIVE: a Homeric synonym for "Greek"

ARGUS: a hundred-eyed monster slain by Hermes

ARTEMIS: virginal goddess of hunting and the moon

ASCRA: hometown of the Greek poet Hesiod and setting for his inspiration from the Muses

ASIA: a term used by the ancient Greeks to refer to present-day Turkey

ASTYANAX: son of Hector and Andromache

ATALANTA: swift-footed young woman who eluded suitors by outracing and then killing them

ATHENA: Greek goddess of wisdom and intelligence

ATHENS: setting for Greece's most intensely creative cultural epoch, the fifth century B.C.E.

ATREUS: father of Agamemnon and Menelaus, leaders of the Greek expedition to Troy

ATTIS: handsome youth beloved by Cybele

BACCHUS: Greek god of wine and ecstasy, also known as Dionysus

BATHYLLUS: sweetheart of an anonymous young woman who ordered his portrait painted

CAESAR: originally, "Julius" Caesar, the Roman general and dictator

CALABRIA: a region in southern Italy, the "toe" of the Italian "boot"

CALYPSO: Greek goddess who fell in love with Odysseus and tried to detain him on her island

CANOPUS: a city in the Nile delta famed for its temple of Serapis

CARIA: a region in ancient western Turkey

CARTHAGE: a North African kingdom founded by Dido, and a later rival of Rome

CENTAUR: a mythological creature half-human and half-horse

CERBERUS: three-headed watchdog who guarded the entrance to the Land of the Dead

CERES: Roman goddess of grain and earthly fertility

CHIRON: a wise centaur who was appointed young Achilles' tutor

CHLOE: a name for a young sweetheart of Horace

CILICIA(NS): a region (and people) located in southeastern Turkey

CORINNA: a pseudonym for Ovid's mistress

CORINTH: a Greek city on the isthmus connecting southern and northern Greece

CRANAE: the Mediterranean island where Paris and Helen stopped on their way to Troy

CRETE: the largest of the islands of Greece, located south of the mainland

CUPID(s): the son of Venus, sometimes conceptualized in multiple forms; synonymous with Eros

CYBELE: Near Eastern earth- and mother-goddess

CYPRIS: another name for Aphrodite, derived from Cyprus, a center of her worship

CYPRUS: Mediterranean island famed for its worship of Aphrodite

CYTHERIA: another name for Aphrodite, from Cythera, the island where she rose from the sea

CYNTHIA: a pseudonym for Propertius' mistress

DEMOSTHENES: renowned Athenian orator

DIDO: queen of Carthage who became enamored of Aeneas

DIONYSUS: Greek god of wine and ecstasy, also known as Bacchus

EËTION: father of Andromache

EPICURUS: famous Greek philosopher who argued that pleasure should be life's greatest aim

EROS: Greek god of sexual attraction and love (hence "erotic"); synonymous with Cupid

EURYDICE: a young woman loved and lost by the musician Orpheus

FATES: three Greek goddesses who determined the destiny of mortals

FURIUS: an acquaintance of Catullus

GLYCERA: a girlfriend of Martial (from the Greek word for "sweet"; hence "Sweetie")

GRACES: three goddesses of beauty and charm, portrayed as lovely young women

HADES: god who ruled over the ghosts of the dead; also a name for his realm

HECATE: a mysterious goddess associated with darkness and witchcraft

HECTOR: bravest of the warriors of Troy and husband of Andromache

HECUBA: queen of Troy and mother of Hector

HELEN: wife of Menelaus, Sparta's king; paramour of Paris and cause of the Trojan war

HELIOS: Greek god of the sun

HEPHAESTUS: Greek god of craftsmanship and metallurgy

HERCULES: the renowned strongman of Greek mythology, famed for his twelve successful "labors"

HERMES: the Greek messenger god

HYPEREIA: a freshwater spring in southern Greece

IDOMENEUS: warrior who fought on the Greek side during the Trojan War

IONIA: region of Greek colonies on the west coast of ancient Turkey

ISIS: Egyptian goddess and wife of Osiris; with him ruled over the Egyptian land of the dead

ISTHMUS: specifically, the Isthmus of Corinth that connected southern and northern Greece

JUNO: queen of the Roman gods; enemy of Aeneas and the divine plan to found Rome

LAERTES: father of Odysseus

LAIS: famous Greek courtesan

LAMPUS: one of the horses ("Bright") that, with Phaëthon ("Shining"), drew the Sun's chariot

LEMNOS: an island off the west coast of Turkey

LESBIA: pseudonym for Catullus' mistress

LESBOS: island birthplace of Sappho

LETHE: the river of forgetfulness in the Land of the Dead

LYCORIS: one of Martial's sweethearts

MAIONIA: a region in central Turkey also known as Lydia

MEDEA: a foreign princess famed for her knowledge of sorcery

MEMPHIS: a city in Egypt

MENANDER: author of Greek comedies

MENELAUS: king of Sparta and husband of Helen

MESSEIS: a freshwater spring in southern Greece

MILANION: suitor and, later, husband of Atalanta

MOUNT OLYMPUS: tallest mountain in Greece; home of the Greek gods

MOUNT PLACUS: a mountain of unknown location in ancient Turkey

MUSES: divine patronesses of the arts

ODYSSEUS: hero of Homer's *Odyssey*

OLYMPUS: the mountain on whose summit the Greek gods dwelled

ORPHEUS: a musician who descended into Hades to rescue the soul of his beloved Eurydice

OSIRIS: Egyptian god of fertility and eternal life

PANDION: an Athenian king, father of Procne and Philomela

PAPHOS: a city on the west coast of Cyprus famed for its temple dedicated to Aphrodite

PARIAN: from the island of Paros, famed for its white marble

PARIS: lover of Helen "of Troy"; a Trojan prince also called Alexander

PARTHENIA: the name of a maid who served Propertius' mistress, Cynthia

PARTHIA: a country southeast of the Caspian Sea famed for its warriors skilled in archery

PENELOPE: faithful wife of Odysseus

PERSEUS: a hero who rescued Andromeda from a dragon that held her captive

PHAËTHON: one of the two horses that pulled the chariot of the Sun

PHAROS: an island just north of the Nile delta

PHOEBUS: an epithet ("Bright" or "Radiant") of the god Apollo

PHOENICIA: the ancient name of Lebanon, a land famed in antiquity for its merchants and mariners

PHRYGIA(NS): a region (and people) located in central Turkey

PLACUS: a site of unknown location in ancient Turkey

PLATO: famous Greek philosopher, student of Socrates and teacher of Aristotle

POLLUX: one of heroic twin sons (the other being Castor) of the god Jupiter

POSEIDON: Greek god of the sea and of earthquakes

PRIAM: king of Troy

PROTESILAUS: a Greek warrior who, after his death, was permitted by the gods to revisit his wife

PYGMALION: the man who fell in love with the statue he had carved

RHODES: a sun-drenched island off the coast of Turkey

ROME: the capital of the ancient Roman Empire; founded by Romulus

ROMULUS: legendary founder of Rome; nurtured with his twin brother, Remus, by a she-wolf

SABINE: a tribe that inhabited territory bordering the site of Rome

SAMOS: an island off the southwestern coast of Turkey

SCAMANDRIUS: an alternate name for Astyanax, the son of Hector and Andromache

SCAEAN GATE: the city of Troy's main gate

SCYTHIA: a country in eastern Europe or western Asia inhabited by warring nomads

SEMIRAMIS: a sensuous Babylonian queen

SEVEN SAGES: seven legendary wise men of early Greece

SINTIANS: a Thracian people who had settled on the island of Lemnos

SPARTA: hometown of Helen and Menelaus

STHENELAIS: a courtesan mentioned in *The Greek Anthology*

SULPICIUS, SERVIUS: patrician uncle of the poet Sulpicia

SYCHAEUS: deceased husband of queen Dido of Carthage

TANTALUS: Lydian king eternally punished for his arrogance by Zeus

THEBE: a city in ancient Turkey

THESEUS: Athenian hero who slew the Minotaur and went on to become Athens' king

THRACE: region east of Macedonia bordering the Black Sea

THRACIA: another name for Thrace

TIPHYS: captain of the ship that transported the Argonauts on their mission

TIVOLI: hilltop town sixteen miles northeast of Rome, where many Roman nobles built their villas

TROJANS: the people of Troy who fought against the Greeks in the Trojan War

TROY: a rich and highly fortified city on the west coast of Turkey; site of the Trojan War

TYRIAN: named for the Phoenician city of Tyre, famed for its rich purple dye

TYDEUS: father of the Greek warrior Diomedes

VENUS: Roman goddess of sexual attraction and love; called Aphrodite by the Greeks

ZEUS: king of the Greek gods; known to the Romans as Jupiter

RECOMMENDED READING

Readers wishing to consult the original Greek and Latin texts of the poems included in this anthology may conveniently turn to the *Loeb Classical Library* published by Harvard University Press, a series of works that features the ancient text and a literal English translation of that text on opposite pages. Readers wishing to fully explore in translation the work of any major ancient poet should turn to the many volumes available in Signet and Penguin editions.

THE ANCIENT NEAR EAST

ANCIENT EGYPT

Foster, John R. *Hymns, Prayers, and Songs: An Anthology of Ancient Egyptian Lyric Poetry.* Atlanta: Scholars Press, 1995.
———. *Love Songs of the New Kingdom.* New York: Scribner's Sons, 1974.
Manniche, Lise. *Sexual Life in Ancient Egypt.* New York: Columbia University Press, 1987.
O'Connor, David. "Eros in Egypt." In *Archaeology Odyssey*, Sept/Oct 2001, 42–51.
Pound, Ezra and Noel Stock. *Come Swiftly to Your Love: Love Poems of Ancient Egypt.* New York: New Directions, 1962; Kansas City, MO: Hallmark, 1971.

ANCIENT MESOPOTAMIA

Bertman, Stephen. *Handbook to Life in Ancient Mesopotamia.* New York: Facts On File, 2003, 180–82, 184 ("Erotic Poetry").
Jacobsen, Thorkild. *The Harps That Once . . . : Sumerian Poetry in Translation.* New Haven, CT: Yale University Press, 1997.
Leick, Gwendolyn. *Sex and Eroticism in Mesopotamian Literature.* New York: Routledge, 1994.
Wolkstein, Diane and Samuel Noah Kramer. *Inana: Queen of Heaven and Earth: Her Stories and Hymns from Sumer.* New York: Harper & Row, 1983.

ANCIENT ISRAEL

Bloch, Chana and Ariel. *The Song of Songs: A New Translation with an Introduction and Commentary*. Berkeley: University of California Press, 1998.
Fox, Michael. *The Song of Songs and Ancient Egyptian Love Songs*. Madison: University of Wisconsin Press, 1985.

CLASSICAL CIVILIZATION

GENERAL

Bertman, Stephen. "The Ashes and the Flame: Passion and Aging in Classical Poetry." In *Old Age in Greek and Latin Literature,* Thomas M. Falkner and Judith de Luce, eds. Albany: State University of New York Press, 1989, 157–71.
Cantarella, Eva. *Bisexuality in the Ancient World*. Second ed. New Haven, CT: Yale University Press, 2002.
Edwards, Mark W. *Sound, Sense, and Rhythm: Listening to Greek and Latin Poetry*. Princeton, NJ: Princeton University Press, 2004.
Highet, Gilbert. *The Classical Tradition*. New York: Oxford University Press, 1949.
Hubbard, Thomas K., ed. *Homosexuality in Greece and Rome*. Berkeley: University of California Press, 2003.
McClure, Laura K., ed. *Sexuality and Gender in the Classical World*. Malden, MA, and Oxford: Blackwell, 2002.
Nussbaum, Martha C. and Juha Sihvola. *The Sleep of Reason: Erotic Experience and Sexual Ethics in Ancient Greece and Rome*. Chicago: University of Chicago Press, 2002.

ANCIENT GREECE

Burn, A. R. *The Lyric Age of Greece*. New York: St. Martin's Press, 1967.
Dover, Kenneth. *Greek Homosexuality*. rev. ed. Cambridge, MA: Harvard University Press, 1989.
———, et al, eds. *Ancient Greek Literature*. Second ed. New York: Oxford University Press, 1997.
Faraone, Christopher A. *Ancient Greek Love Magic*. Cambridge, MA: Harvard University Press, 1999.
Greene, Ellen. *Reading Sappho: Contemporary Approaches*. Berkeley: University of California Press, 1999.

———. *Reading Sappho: Reception and Transmission.* Berkeley: University of California Press, 1999.

Licht, Hans. *Sexual Life in Ancient Greece.* London: Abbey Library, 1932.

Powell, Barry B. *Classical Myth.* Englewood Cliffs, NJ: Prentice Hall, 1995.

Rayor, Diane. *Sappho's Lyre: Archaic Lyric and Women Poets of Ancient Greece.* Berkeley: University of California Press, 1991.

Sansone, David. *Ancient Greek Civilization.* Malden, MA, and Oxford: Blackwell, 2003.

Winkler, John J. *The Constraints of Desire: The Anthropology of Sex and Gender in Ancient Greece.* New York: Routledge, 1989.

ANCIENT ROME

Armstrong, David. *Horace.* New Haven, CT: Yale University Press, 1989.

Clarke, John R. *Roman Sex: 100 B.C.–A.D. 250.* New York: Abrams, 2003.

Cockayne, Karen. *Experiencing Old Age in Ancient Rome.* New York: Routledge, 2003, ch. 6, "Sexuality."

Grant, Michael and Antonia Mulas. *Eros in Pompeii: The Secret Rooms of the National Museum of Naples.* New York: Morrow, 1975.

Hardie, Philip, ed. *The Cambridge Companion to Ovid.* New York: Cambridge University Press, 2002.

Kiefer, Otto. *Sexual Life in Ancient Rome.* London: Abbey Library, 1934.

Luck, Georg. *The Latin Love Elegy.* Second ed. London: Methuen, 1969.

Martin, Charles. *Catullus.* New Haven, CT: Yale University Press, 1992.

Mendell, Clarence W. *Latin Poetry: The New Poets and the Augustans.* New Haven, CT: Yale University Press, 1965.

Quinn, Kenneth. *The Catullan Revolution.* Ann Arbor: University of Michigan Press, 1959.

Sullivan, J. P. *Propertius: A Critical Introduction.* New York: Cambridge University Press, 1976.

Thibault, J. C. *The Mystery of Ovid's Exile.* Berkeley: University of California Press, 1964.

Williams, Craig A. *Roman Homosexuality: Ideologies of Masculinity in Classical Antiquity.* New York: Oxford University Press, 1999.

ABOUT THE AUTHOR

Stephen Bertman is Professor Emeritus of Classical Studies at Canada's University of Windsor. He holds a doctorate in Greek and Latin from Columbia University, and additional degrees in Near Eastern and Judaic Studies and Classics from Brandeis University and New York University. His books on the ancient world include *Art and the Romans, The Conflict of Generations in Ancient Greece and Rome, Doorways Through Time: The Romance of Archaeology, Handbook to Life in Ancient Mesopotamia*, and *Climbing Olympus: What You Can Learn from Greek Myth and Wisdom*. In addition to writing about the ancient Mediterranean world, Dr. Bertman has also explored the challenges of contemporary American society in *Hyperculture: The Human Cost of Speed* and *Cultural Amnesia: America's Future and the Crisis of Memory*. He has also been a frequent guest on radio interview shows in the United States and Canada. Dr. Bertman lives with his wife, Elaine, in West Bloomfield, Michigan.